Praise for
Did the Government Write Your Will?

"Eric Gullotta cuts through the complexities and makes it possible to navigate the maze of estate planning in such a way that you can find the reasons and motivation to get your estate in order. I recommend *Did The Government Write Your Will?* and his principles. With the use of real life examples, Eric not only makes it interesting but clearly illustrates the pros and cons of the typical approaches of dealing with our estate. Eric is a sharp practitioner. If you are interested in making smart choices about your estate, you need this book."

—**Montgomery Taylor, CPA, RIA, CRDS, author of *Before It's Too Late and The New Rules of Success***

"Eric presents an excellent summary of the laws and procedures surrounding settlement of estates. While one should always consult with an attorney, this book gives a readable overview of probate and estate administration law that varies between 'light' to make it interesting and 'solid,' with great information for the average reader."

—**Malcolm Manwell, estate planning attorney; partner at Perry, Johnson, Anderson, Miller and Moskowitz**

"Eric Gullotta is an estate planning attorney who really understands what he is talking about. Estate planning is one of the main procrastination points for clients. It is about our mortality and what happens to our stuff after we are gone, which makes it easy to put on the back burner. In his book, *Did the Government Write Your Will?*, Eric walks you through what happens if you don't make decisions and explains in clear terms what some of the decision points are if you choose to take action. You can read it in an hour; you should keep it on your shelf, right next to your estate plan, so you can reference your wise decision."

—Charles Daniels III, financial planner; principal at Harvest Financial, LLC

"Eric Gullotta presents compelling reasons to have your estate planning documents prepared and 'disinherit' the government's will. You have worked hard for your money; decide for yourself how you want it to be distributed upon your death. This is a must-read for anyone who is wondering why they need a will or a revocable trust."

—Jennifer Hainstock, estate planning attorney

Did the Government Write Your Will?

Eric Gullotta, Esq.

Gullotta Law Group

For more information visit www.GullottaLaw.com

Printed in the United States of America

Did the Government Write Your Will?
Eric Gullotta, Esq.

1. Title   2. Author   3. Law / Estate Planning

Library of Congress Control Number: 2014933709
ISBN: 978-0-615-97266-4

To my parents, Richard and Lucille Gullotta. Without them this book as well as my career would not have been possible.

To my family, whom I work tirelessly for everyday, but most importantly to my amazing wife, Lani, who consistently inspires me with her love, hard work, and wonderful spirit.

Table of Contents

CHAPTER 1

Introduction to Estate Planning in California

A s an attorney whose practice focuses on estate planning, I work with people to ensure that their final wishes are carried out with regard to their assets. Over the years, I have found that the vast majority of people don't actually understand what happens when they die *intestate*, or without a will. Therefore, I often play the role of educator as well as counselor. I present my clients with estate planning options—whether that means drawing up a will, setting up a trust, or simply making a gift while they are still alive; I also explain what will happen if, in the absence of such planning, the government distributes their assets according to the default statutory rules of succession. Once armed with this information, most people decide to opt out of the so-called "government will." Unfortunately, others put off planning until it is too late.

Lynn, a sixty-five-year-old woman, had come to see me a number of times about estate planning. She suffered from health conditions that in all likelihood would cut her life short, and she thought she should prepare a will or, as she put it, "one of those other things." I think she was referring to a trust.

Lynn was divorced and had two children—a daughter with whom she was extremely close, and a son who…well, let's just say he wasn't going to be named "son of the year" anytime soon. Lynn's wishes regarding her assets were simple and specific: she wanted everything to go to her daughter. Yet, at the same time, she was terrified of making this decision permanent; perhaps she felt guilty disinheriting her son, despite the way he treated her. I wasn't sure. But I did know that even after several discussions, she continued to operate under the assumption that things would simply work out in the end.

When I didn't hear from Lynn for a while, I became concerned and called to check up on her. She admitted that she was still having a hard time making her decision final and that she was "scared" to make a will. That's when I explained that she already *had* a will—the one guaranteed her by the government. If she were to die without drafting her own documents, her assets would be distributed according to statute rather than her individual wishes. This did the trick; Lynn agreed to do estate planning, just as soon as she helped her daughter through a painful divorce. Unfortunately, Lynn passed away in the middle of the divorce proceedings with no estate plan in place.

Although Lynn's death was untimely, she had been aware of the risks. This arguably gave her the advantage over many others who believe (sometimes erroneously) that they have long lives ahead of them. However, her reluctance to commit to an estate plan resulted in her daughter receiving half of what she intended her to have (under the intestacy laws, her son would inherit the same amount as her daughter regardless of Lynn's relationship with him).

Lynn's story illustrates how important it is not only to know the facts about estate planning and to act on them in a timely manner but to do so without fear. Although she was on the fence about having a will, she very clearly articulated to me her desire to leave everything to her daughter. That desire is irrelevant, however, to the probate court. My purpose in writing in this book is to provide as many people as possible with current, competent, and correct information so they can take a proactive role in the distribution of their assets.

Preparing an estate plan is favored by everyone involved, including the judges who oversee estates. Courts are already overburdened with unnecessary proceedings for the administration of estates. The judges, and the counties they work in, would run much more efficiently if people avoided probate by using wills and revocable trusts. That would cut down on routine paperwork and allow courts to concentrate on more important issues, such as elder abuse, contested wills and trusts, or disputes among beneficiaries.

Remember that most judges are also attorneys; therefore, they understand how necessary and important estate planning is, not to mention economically prudent. Estate planning costs money "up front," but it saves your estate time and money in the long run. It also saves your loved ones the heartache involved with red tape and court battles after you're gone. Think of it as preventative medicine.

I know what you're thinking right now—that what happened to Lynn would never happen to you. Perhaps you're in great health and think that Lynn should have been more on top of things, considering her medical problems. You may be thinking that what happened to her is a rare occurrence. But that is simply not the case. In April 2013, *Forbes* ran an article about Roman Blum, a Holocaust survivor who had recently died intestate in New York. Blum had no children, and his wife had predeceased him by more than a decade. So why did his death merit an article in *Forbes*? Because his entire estate, all *$40 million* of it, will probably go to the Empire State! Here is an excerpt from that article:

> Nearly 2.5 million Americans died last year,
> many without signing a will. One of them

was apparently Roman Blum, a Holocaust survivor and New York real estate developer, who was worth almost $40 million when he passed away in January 2012 at the age of 97. A worldwide search for heirs since then hasn't turned up any living relatives. If, after three years, there's still no sign of his doing any estate planning and no one comes forward to claim his assets, all that money will go to New York State, under a legal rule called escheat.

You can read the colorful details of Blum's life in Julie Satow's New York Times article, "He Left a Fortune, to No One." These are the estate planning lessons that emerge from between the lines.

Another title for this story might have been "It Happens to the Best of Us." Mr. Blum was undoubtedly a sophisticated person, yet he still failed to prepare an estate plan. Now, I didn't know the man, but I would venture to guess that while he didn't have any relatives, he probably would have preferred that a worthy charity receive his estate rather than the State of New York.

You have many options when it comes to preparing your estate plan. You can purchase one of a dozen do-it-yourself estate planning programs or use free advice from the Internet. But while these measures might be valid in a court of law, they are also the legal equivalent of performing your own root canal. That's why the best option is *always* to seek the advice of competent legal counsel in your state of residency.

That said, this book is not intended to be a self-help or instruction manual. Instead, I like to think of it as an informal discussion to help you begin thinking about estate planning. You won't find a lot of confusing legalese; the idea is for regular folks to understand the importance of preparing estate documents. This book is also meant to motivate. By providing you with the knowledge you deserve, it gives you the tools to decide for yourself whether you want the government to control the distribution of your estate.

Every state has its own laws when it comes to estate distribution. As I am licensed only in California, I focus on the rules of that state. However, I also reference the Uniform Probate Code (UPC), which is what many state laws are based on. The UPC is a comprehensive body of law that unifies, clarifies, and modernizes the laws governing the affairs of decedents and their estates, including wills and other instruments, such as trusts. No matter where you live, the moment you were born, the government, whether state or federal, wrote your will. It is up to you to opt out of it.

Before we begin, I must remind you that this book is not legal advice. We have not created an attorney-client relationship. Anything said in this book should be researched and confirmed by an attorney or other competent professional. Now, on to the good stuff!

CHAPTER 2

What Is a Government Will, and Why Do I Have One?

S ince the beginning of time, people have been concerned with how their assets will be distributed after they die. Of course, things were simpler in ancient times, when real estate wasn't owned and the most valuable possessions were the tools men used for hunting and gathering, which they passed on to their eldest sons or tribal elders.

There were also societies that buried the wealthy with their prized possessions so they could enjoy them in the afterlife. That made estate planning very simple!

As early as 800 BC, ancient Greeks began recognizing property rights apart from the government; this might be the earliest signs of recognized independent property ownership. In feudal times, the flow of property was controlled by the sovereign, who parceled it out in return for fealty and service. It was a military system established in Europe after the decline of the Roman Empire. These allotments were known as "feoda," "feuds," "fiefs," or "fees." The holder of the feud was said to be "enfeoffed."

The manner of enfeofment was as follows: first, a vassal pledged his homage to the lord (a person of noble blood). This was a ceremony in which the vassal entered into submission to his lord and became his "man" (basically, vassals were considered no better than slaves). After the homage came an oath of fealty, followed by the transfer of the land. That all changed in the early 1800s, when the Napoleonic Code introduced the notion of absolute ownership. Since then, things have grown increasingly complex. Our modern form of government was born and, with it, the government will.

The point of this history lesson is to show that throughout history, every society has had means of distributing its citizens' assets after they die. It is in the public interest to have a system where a person's possessions are dispersed in an orderly fashion. It goes to the heart of why we have *any* laws: essentially, differences in opinion, often resulting in conflict, are part of the human condition. That's why we need a uniform body of rules that either prevents conflicts or resolves them peacefully. We couldn't have fighting in the streets every time someone died, could we? So we went from agreed-upon practices among tribesmen to codified, prescribed laws stating exactly how things will be distributed—whether you like it or not.

I am not disputing the need for the government's default plan (also known as intestate succession). Without this plan, there would be no rules about what would happen to our stuff after we die. An unorganized and chaotic scheme just wouldn't work. While certain items could be discarded, others must be cared for in order to prevent great harm to those around us—even the public at large. Imagine that the owner of a nuclear power plant died without any instruction on how it was to be handled or controlled. Without an owner, the employees would walk away since salaries are no longer being paid. With no employees manning the switches, the fuel rods overheat and—voila!—thermonuclear detonation (or something like that...remember, I am an attorney, not a nuclear scientist!). Am I going little overboard? Perhaps, but you see what I mean.

Everyone needs to be subject to some default rule. Even infants need a way to dispose of their possessions or wealth. Yes, even infants can have assets, usually the proceeds of some sort of legal suit (i.e., due to a birth defect or medical issue). Or perhaps an infant was killed in a car accident or burned by a defective product. That infant's parents or a guardian ad litem will bring suit on behalf of the infant. If the infant's estate recovers, who gets the money? In most cases, it's the infant's parents, but, again, these sorts of details must be worked out under the law. The bottom line is that no matter who you are, what age you are, or where you are in life, there may come a time when your possessions will need to be distributed in an orderly manner. If you don't choose the means of distribution, your estate will be parceled up by the probate court according to the government's rules. This is what I always explain to my clients: when you avoid making a decision, you are actually choosing to subject your estate—and your intended beneficiaries—to the whims of these default schemes. These schemes are substandard and can potentially drain your assets in the form of court and attorney fees.

Like my client Lynn, many people are hesitant or flat out refuse to make a legal declaration regarding the distribution of their assets. I have heard dozens of reasons for this, but there are a few constants. Some people, for example, worry that the will or trust instrument won't be perfect or that their circumstances will change and it won't be perfect anymore. Others are superstitious—they feel that if they make a will, it will bring about their deaths. Still others feel that their assets aren't valuable enough to warrant estate planning. Whatever the case, the truth is that a will is arguably the most important legal document a person can have. Why? Because it is the last time you will be able to communicate your wishes. This isn't like drawing up a contract, when you are around to explain yourself after the fact. Once you're dead, that's it; there are no extensions or do-overs. Your will ensures that your loved ones receive what you want them to receive and not what the government wants them to get.

Now that we covered the history and purpose of the government will, let's move on to how it operates, independent of your personal wishes.

CHAPTER 3

What's in the Government Will?

The purpose of this chapter is to spur you into action by teaching you about the default provisions of the government will. I think, like most of my clients, you'll find that these default terms are ineffective, costly, and often cause undue to hardship to the decedent's loved ones.

I'm always surprised when people come into my office with no idea of what is going to happen when they die. Or, even worse, somebody has already died, and his or her family members have no idea what's supposed to happen next. You'd think that this is the sort of thing people would consider before it was too late. But as I speak with them, I often find that they spent more time planning a road trip or vacation than they did the distribution of their assets to their children. It may sound morbid, but the fact is that even while on that road trip, you're still around to change direction, make new decisions, or just go with the flow, whereas when you're dead, you can't make decisions on the fly. Your previous decisions, for better or worse, are now set in stone, and your family members are left dealing with the consequences. That's why you have to make sure your final wishes are clearly stated in a will, trust, or other legally binding instrument.

First, though, I think it makes sense to define a few terms, starting with "probate." Probate is the process whereby the court manages an estate. Remember that each state has its own rules concerning probate; I'm focusing on California, in which most probate cases are managed under the Independent Administration of Estates Act. This empowers the executor of the estate to handle most of the estate's business without permission from the court. (There are some things that do require court permission—more on that later.)

After someone passes away, the first step for the court is to determine whether the decedent's will was valid or if he or she died without one. If the decedent had a valid will and named a specific executor or administrator then that person is empowered to pay bills and handle other transactions on behalf of the estate once appointed by the court. If the person did not have a will then the court will appoint someone, usually a close relative of the decedent, to serve as administrator. There are also certain circumstances when the court must appoint someone even if there was a will (e.g., the person named in the will has passed away or refuses to serve as executor).

After the matter of the executor/administrator has been cleared up, the next step is to take care of any debts. This includes any taxes owed to the government. It's only after these debts have been paid that the money goes to the decedent's beneficiaries. Who these beneficiaries are often depends on whether you're using the government will or your own.

It's important to note here that there are certain assets that are not subject to probate; there are also ways to avoid probate altogether. I'll cover those specific assets later.

For now, let's start with the simplest testamentary instrument: the will.

will, *n.*
a. A legal declaration of how a person wishes his or her possessions to be disposed of after death
b. A legally executed document containing this declaration

As I mentioned above, your will, by definition, is your chance to make your final wishes known. When you die without a will, you have died intestate, thereby activating the government will. Unlike your will, it has an objective view of fairness with no regard to the individual wishes of the decedent. The government has no ability to determine whether you wanted to disinherit one of your children or leave all your money to the cat; moreover, it has no interest in finding out.

It is a fundamental legal right—and, dare I say, a fundamental human right—to pass on your possessions as you see fit. I am not criticizing the government for providing us with a default will because, as we have already established, it is necessary to maintain order in society. However, I do criticize the government for not properly educating the public about it. Everyone should know about the default scheme that dictates who gets their things when they die; they should also know about the often exorbitant fees that can eat away at the estate. We are taught many basic (and arguably much less useful) facts in school, but nowhere is there a class about how to plan for your death or the consequences of failing to take action. That's why I am so passionate about providing people with the ABCs of estate planning, and I have found that once they have all the facts, the vast majority opt to create their own wills rather than relying on the government's.

Some people point out to me that estate planning costs money, while a government will distributes your assets for free. But that is not really the case. Sure, you'll spend some money up front on estate planning (remember the preventative medicine analogy); however, you must look at an estate plan as an investment. If I told you that you could invest three thousand dollars in an estate plan and that the invest-ment was guaranteed to grow to $26,000 (tax free), would you do it? Probably. Well, that is what an estate plan can do for you depending on your assets. It takes the cost of the estate plan and grows it five to ten times in savings (or more, depending on how much you own when you die). Money that would have gone to the courts or your attorney will instead go to your kids or anyone else you choose. Sounds like a great idea.

After hearing this, most people decide immediately to draft an estate plan; others see things a bit differently. A few years ago, a client came into my office with a relatively simple estate. She had two pieces of property, one lower in value than the other. My client wanted the more expensive piece of property to go to her son, who happened to be present at that very meeting and was sitting right next to her. As I do with all my client's who are on the fence about the gov-ernment will, I explained how the intestacy laws work and told her that in order to distribute her property as intended, she would have to opt out and create a different estate plan. After I was finished, she had only one question: how much would estate planning cost her? When I gave her my fee, well, let's just say she was displeased. I calmly looked at her and said, "I know it seems like a lot of money, but you'll save at least that much by avoiding probate. You'll also be able to ensure that your son receives what you want him to receive."

I was rather shocked when she looked me dead in the

eye and said, "Honey, *I* won't be saving *anything* because *I'll* be *dead*." Fortunately for the estate, cooler heads prevailed (and by cooler heads, I mean her son, who would benefit from the estate plan). He paid for his mother's estate plan, which turned out to be a great investment for him.

The specifics of intestate distribution depend upon the state in which you live. Every state is different, so I can't tell you exactly what your government will say if you live outside California. However, as I said earlier, most states based their laws on the Uniform Probate Code (UPC). The UPC governs intestacy with the following simplified rules.[1]

1. If you are survived by a spouse but do not have children or parents, your spouse gets everything.
2. If you are married and have kids but those kids are with your surviving spouse, the spouse *still* gets everything (as long as the surviving spouse has no descendants who are not descendants of the decedent)
3. If you are not married and do not have children then your parents inherit; if your parents are deceased then your siblings inherit. If there are no siblings then the court checks for other relations—aunts, uncles, and cousins, no matter how distant.

---

1. Uniform Probate Code, last updated 2006.

This doesn't sound so bad, right? Well, no, if your desires happen to fall within this very narrow formula. But what if you have a spouse and children but also want to leave money to your sibling or your best friend since the first grade? Or if you wanted to leave a sizable contribution to your favorite charity? What if you have a significant other to whom you are not married but would like to provide for? If so, the government will is not for you. Instead of your friend or charity, some distant cousin who you didn't like or never even met might get your estate.

And if you think *that's* bad...

4. If you have no living relatives, your entire estate escheats to the state. Remember the case of Mr. Blum, whose $40-million estate will go to the State of New York unless they find relatives within three years.

5. Your government will also leaves part of your estate to your attorney. Whoa...what? Those guys are already rich and don't need any more money! How could the government do that? Well, it is based on the reasonable-compensation clause of the UPC and has been codified into law by many states, including California (more on that later).

As troubling as the financial aspect of the government will is, there is something even more important and, arguably, the biggest reason to make your own will. When considering whether to engage in estate planning, you must consider not only what the government will says but also what it *doesn't* say. For example, the government will makes absolutely no provision for where your children will live in the event of your death. Only by opting out, through the use of a will or trust, can you designate who will care for your children. Most people consider their children their most valuable assets; therefore, the fact that the intestacy laws do not provide for their care is a glaring omission. If for no other reason, you should make a will or trust to ensure that if you pass away, your children are cared for by the people of your choice.

So, you see, the government will is based on statute, pure and simple; there is no room for the decedent's personal wishes. However, there is a good reason for this: fairness. While it may seem unfair to ignore an individual's wishes, there must be a system in place that operates in a reliable fashion. Imagine if the government tried to delve into the mind of each decedent before dispensing with his or her assets. Imagine the disputes between feuding family members; imagine the time and resources (i.e., taxpayers' money) that would be needed for such an investigation. It would be chaotic, right? But just because we understand the rationale behind the government will doesn't mean we have to accept it. In chapter four, we'll discuss another reason you should opt out of the government will: it will drain money from your estate.

CHAPTER 4

What Does the Government Will Cost You?

As mentioned in the previous chapter, some people don't have a problem with the government will because they believe it will save them money. And it's true—they will not have to pay an attorney to draft their estate planning documents. If you are one of the lucky few whose wishes are aligned with the rules of intestacy, that's great. However, as I will explain in this chapter, this "free" government will can actually eat away at your estate with a number of expenses, both foreseen and unforeseen. So while you avoid the fee to create estate planning documents, your decedents will pay through the nose after you're gone. How does this happen? The answer is simple: fees, fees, and more fees.

To me, the fees involved with dying intestate can be likened to piranha: when there is only one, it is merely annoying, and, at most, all it will do is nip at you. But when you are surrounded by a swarm, all those nips add up to a big bite. Now instead of simply annoying you, they are doing significant damage. The amounts and types of the fees depend on the complexity of your estate; however, here is a general picture of how fees affect your estate as it goes through the probate process.

COURT COSTS

One of the first questions I ask my clients when they come into my office for a probate consult is, "How is your cash situation?" Usually they look confused/annoyed/suspicious when I ask this because I've just gotten through explaining how attorneys aren't paid until the end of the probate process and, furthermore, that they are paid by the estate, not out of pocket. So at this moment they are probably thinking, *Here we go again—an attorney asking for money.* The truth is that the executor or administrator is responsible for posting the court fee to begin the probate process. In most counties in California, the current filing fee is $465. However, due to the economic climate, counties are cutting back on services and raising fees. In fact, by the time you read this, this fee may actually be more.

It's important to note here that all estates have to go through probate, even when the decedent had a will. Once the estate enters the probate process, it is vulnerable to be eaten away by court costs. However, when you do create a will, you can add certain provisions that help protect your assets, including:

1. **No-contest clause**. A no-contest clause punishes people who challenge a will by writing them out of the will completely. They get nothing. This is definitely a double-edged sword. On one hand, it deters litigation by punishing somebody for bringing an unnecessary or frivolous suit. On the other hand, there are times when people who are just looking for clarification on an estate inadvertently trigger the no-contest clause. That means that anyone who is going to request clarification will have to spend extra money on attorney's fees just to make sure they are administering the estate correctly. Therefore, although a no-contest clause can protect the estate, it often does more harm than good. Like I said, it's a double-edged sword, and there's a good chance you're going to be cut.

2. **Waiver of surety bond**. A surety bond is a bond that is required by the court to protect the estate in the event that the executor decides to steal from it. If the executor steals from the estate, the beneficiaries that would have received money in the will are made whole by the insurance

company (this means the insurance company pays them what they would have received under the will). Sounds great, right? The reality is, however, that in most cases this does not make sense. In most situations, the spouse and/or children of the deceased are going to inherit everything, and they are certainly not going to steal from themselves. If this is the case then requiring an executor or administrator to post this bond is just another unnecessary fee; it wastes the beneficiaries' money and contradicts the spirit of the law that was designed to protect them. By way of example, in San Francisco, California, a $300,000 bond can cost a recent client twelve hundred dollars per year. That means that a probate taking about a year will waste twelve hundred dollars that could've gone to the children of the decedent.

Sometimes, through no fault of the decedent, the probate process is beset by lengthy delays (I'll discuss this bureaucratic red tape in further detail later on). For example, one San Francisco case involved several issues on which I had to work with the county assessor. The delays associated with these issues kept the estate open for almost two years. The cost of the bond ran for that entire period, costing the beneficiaries $2,400 just for the bond. Although all estate planners charge different rates, there is a good chance the client could have paid for a comprehensive estate plan, including a trust, for less than the amount of just the bonding fee. This puts things in a different perspective, right?

3. **Waiver of accounting**. Just like the surety bond discussed above, accountings are oftentimes unnecessary. An accounting means that the person in charge of the money has to account to the beneficiary. If the beneficiary has been in charge of it the whole time, he or she would then have to account to himself or herself. Accountings are expensive and time-consuming; they are also more a matter of course than a matter of necessity. For example, let's say the decedent's two children are going to inherit the entire estate. Although they would never steal from themselves, as co-executors, they are responsible to pay for an accounting. This is performed by an accounting firm and costs thousands of dollars. However, by adding a simple provision to your will, the accounting can be waived either completely or by the majority of beneficiaries, thus saving them both time and money.

4. **Independent executor powers**. In California, the Independent Administration of Estates Act grants the executor the power to act on the estate's

behalf without court approval. When the executor has full authority, this includes the ability to sell real estate and personal properly. Without independent administrative executor powers, however, the executor and his or her attorney are required to go to court to get this approval; this is both a cumbersome and expensive process and should therefore be avoided whenever possible.

ATTORNEY COSTS

As I mentioned above, the government will leaves a healthy sum of your money to your attorney. Now you might be thinking, *Wait a minute—why would I need an attorney when the government is distributing my assets?* Well, the UPC, as well as many state laws (including those of California), has statutory attorney's fees. Statutory fees in California happen to be among the highest in the country and are based on the value of the estate (other states, including Nevada and Wyoming, have also adopted fee schedules based on the size of the estate). Not surprisingly, these fees can be much higher than the typical attorney's hourly rate.

So, basically, whether you hire an attorney to help you with estate planning or you die intestate and your children hire an attorney, there will be attorney's fees. It's just a question of when they are paid and by whom. Will it be you in an attorney's office? Or will it be your children, whose inheritance is whittled away by the government will?

The value of your estate is actually a tricky thing to figure out; it seems even more so because most people don't realize how it's calculated. In California, the gross value of all probate assets are added together, which sounds simple enough; however, the total value is not reduced by the amount for any debts owed, which is a common misconception.

It only gets more complicated from there. You then add any gains realized on personal or real property sold during the administration of the estate and are allowed to subtract any losses from disposed or sold property as well. This requires an accounting to the court, which can be a major headache.

It is important to note here that there are assets—usually custodial type accounts, such as IRAs (individual retirement accounts), life insurance, annuities, and other types of retirement accounts—that are not subject to the probate process. There are also certain pieces of real estate (i.e., those you hold as joint tenants) that don't need to go through probate. In the case of joint tenancy, when one of the tenants dies, the title passes, by operation of law, to the other joint tenant (i.e., the person named on the deed). This is called "the right of survivorship," and I will talk about it more later; for now, it's sufficient to note that these types of assets are not included in the calculation of the gross estate. Now that we know what we can add, let's look at what we can subtract. The answer is simple: nothing (except losses on real estate or other property). Although the forms ask about the debts of the estate when calculating the gross value (for purposes of figuring out statutory fees), you do not reduce that amount for debt. For example, if you have a house that's been valued at $500,000 but has a $600,000 mortgage on it (which was commonplace after the housing market collapse in 2008), you will actually be paying probate fees on $500,000, even though the estate is insolvent. An even more tragic example would be an estate with a $500,000 piece of property and $485,000 worth of debt. In that case, when the estate property is sold for $500,000 (and after the debts are paid off), there is only $15,000 left. Guess who gets that $15,000? The attorney! Aren't you glad you're reading this book?

The reason for this is that attorneys have the highest order of priority in an estate—they come before all others, even before relatives or other beneficiaries. Don't forget that attorneys make the laws, and the first thing they did was make sure that they'd always get paid first. Is it any wonder we have such terrible reputations?

To make matters worse, there are actually *two* types of attorney compensation. The first is the ordinary compensation we just discussed, which is based on the gross value of the estate. The other is called "extraordinary" fees.

Extraordinary fees are guided by California statute but

are open to interpretation. It is never advisable to leave something open to interpretation when an attorney is involved (and this is coming from an attorney!). However, there are certain circumstances that have been determined to warrant these extraordinary fees, most notably the selling of real estate.

It is very common for real estate to be sold during the probate process; usually it's the personal residence of the decedent. This happens for a few different reasons. Perhaps there is a loan on the property and the lender will not assign it to the heirs. Or it may be because other creditors need to be satisfied and the only real asset in the probate is the house. Another common reason is that the beneficiaries just don't get along. Titling real estate in the name of multiple beneficiaries can be problematic; in fact, depending on the people involved, it can be a recipe for disaster. This is a great reason to opt out rather than accept the government will. If, for example, your children do not get along, you would know better than to put all their names on the house. If it's left up to the probate court, however, your estate will be divvied up according to the rules of intestacy, meaning that each of your children would get an equal share. That's why most attorneys will advise the personal representative of the estate to sell the property when beneficiaries are not getting along.

Unfortunately, this is not always a simple matter.

Beneficiaries can either contest or file petitions against a sale; this causes delays and increases the time the attorney has to spend on the estate (which, of course, equals more fees). In fact, it is entirely possible for huge fights to break out, depending on the beneficiaries and the real estate in question. Most children feel deep, longstanding attachments to the family home and, if at all possible, want to buy it. This is understandable, given the sentimental value and memories of their parents, but it's important to remember that while the parties are busy fighting, the attorneys are getting rich off the estate. Creating your own will can help you avoid this situation, or—even better—you can use a living trust with specific provisions designed to overcome this exact kind of conflict.

Of course, if the property must be sold through probate, the attorney will bill at his or her normal billing rate for any time spent pursuing the sale of the real estate. This includes, but is not limited to, talking to realtors, advising the executor about the sale process, reviewing appraisals, and reviewing sales contracts. This is time-consuming work and warrants extraordinary fees, particularly if the attorney opted, or was forced, to pursue court confirmation of sale.

One instance when an attorney would be forced to seek court confirmation is when there is a large gap between the appraisal and sale amount. Appraisals are subjective and therefore subject to attack. If the property is appraised much higher than the sales price, beneficiaries can allege that the executor breached his or her duty by selling the real estate property too low. However, there may be very real reasons for selling at a lower price. Remember 2008? I had several cases in which someone died in 2007 or 2008 and the real estate had to be sold in 2009 or 2010; every beneficiary (along with every other homeowner in California) was shocked that homes were selling for that little. In fact, during that time period, just about every home sale was contested by one beneficiary or another because they wrongly assumed the low price was due to an error on the part of the executor. The result? They contested the sale, the house sold for the same amount anyway, and my firm charged thousands of dollars in fees to confirm the sale with the court. Sound like something you might want to avoid with your estate?

By seeking court confirmation of sale, the executor protects himself or herself from these allegations of error or wrongdoing. The property is essentially auctioned off in court (it's actually a pretty neat thing to see), which confirms for the court that the highest price for the property was received. Before the auction date, the attorney or executor posts a notice in the paper, notifying people about a court sale of real estate. If you're thinking, *Well, I've never seen that before*, it's because there's a very special niche of real estate buyers that invest in probate sales because of the excellent deals they find.

So why am I talking about a court confirmation of sale? Because it can cost the estate many thousands of dollars in legal fees that could have been avoided. There is a significant amount of work involved in the posting and filing of the documents to request the court confirmation of sale. There is also a potentially lengthy court appearance required. The estate will be billed by the attorney for extraordinary fees on top the ordinary fees. Of course, all of this is unnecessary and can be eliminated by opting out of the government will.

Extraordinary fees are also granted when ancillary probates are involved. Ancillary probates are necessary when there are estate properties in another state and/or multiple states, which means there will be probate proceedings in multiple states. When I am handling this type of estate, I not only charge the regular fees for everything I am handling in California but extraordinary fees for contacting the attorneys who are reviewing out-of-state contracts, requesting certified documents, or any other duties involved with managing the ancillary probates. Again, this is more money going to the attorney that should be going to your kids. I will point out that attorneys are not required to charge the statutory fees, and, in fact, these fees are negotiable. The statutory fee is actually only the *maximum* an attorney can charge. So it stands to reason that an attorney *could* charge less than the full amount to probate an estate. Does it happen very often? No. In fact, it rarely happens, if ever.

While many people might chalk this up to simple greed, there is actually a good reason behind it. Most attorneys who have worked in probate administration know that the fees are merely an estimate; some estates will require more work and others less. Therefore, when a simple estate walks in their door, it is an offset against another, more complicated estate where they are charging the same thing and doing two or three times the work.

By way of example, let's look at two different types of probate cases. Both of these estates have the same gross value, so they would generate the same fee for the attorney. Beneath the surface, however, these estates are very different.

The first estate contained one residence in a large subdivision. The decedent had left the house in wonderful condition. She was survived by her only child, a daughter, who was a finance executive with a large insurance firm. In addition to the residence, there was approximately $250,000 in cash and minimal personal property. We knew from the beginning that the beneficiary wanted to keep the house. As there were sufficient assets other than the house to pay the decedent's final debts, they, along with the remaining cash and personal property, were simply distributed to her daughter. This probate was routine and quick and didn't take up a lot of our time.

The second probate also contained one residence, this one in the mountains. The home had unique characteristics that made it difficult to appraise; it also made it harder to find good buyers. To complicate matters further, the house was the only asset in the estate and was carrying a large mortgage. There was, however, a lot of personal property in the house, and by this I mean the house was packed floor to ceiling. It looked like an episode of *Hoarders*!

The decedent had left everything to her two children, neither of whom should have been put in charge of a house-plant, let alone an estate. Needless to say, preparing the house to be sold so that the debts could be paid was incredibly difficult. The sheer volume of work involved, coupled with the less-than-capable executor, made the situation drag on month after month. Several deals to sell the house fell through at the last minute because of either the location or the condition of the house.

My office spent hours upon hours handling the disposal of the personal property, dealing with the creditors, and eventually having to file a petition with the court to decide which creditors got paid and which didn't. Although we got slight extraordinary fees for the sale of the home, the amount of time we spent on this engagement was far more than our first example above. It is because of situations like these that attorneys rarely reduce their fees. My office has done it on rare occasions, as have other attorneys, but it is the exception rather than the rule so beware of any attorney who says otherwise.

So what will a government will cost you? Well, ironically, the government will is free! You won't pay a cent, but as the saying goes, you get what you pay for. Under the government's poorly drafted and inefficient will, your spouse, children, and any other heirs will pay dearly. When you are paying for each document that needs filing and every moment spent in court, these fees add up very quickly.

OTHER COSTS

While attorney's fees can be calculated based on the value of the estate's gross assets, there are other costs incurred under the government will that cannot be quantified simply by adding up numbers.

I can tell you from personal experience that when estates sell property, they never get the best price. This is because most of the time it is sold in a probate sale per the court confirmation of sale of real estate that we discussed above. The buyers who attend these sales are well aware that the estate is selling an asset in this manner out of necessity. This places the buyer at a great advantage. If you don't believe me, just watch an episode of the reality show *Pawn Stars*; whenever someone is desperate for the money, they're always at a disadvantage when negotiating the price of the item. Well, this is the same principle.

There is a certain sector of the population that frequents probate and estate sales. These are often savvy real estate investors, treasure hunters, or people who just like to collect and sell secondhand goods. Sometimes these goods are bought very cheaply and sold at thrift stores, and sometimes the people going to the sales are looking for valuable items that they can buy cheap and sell high.

Obviously it's frustrating for the beneficiary to sell the real estate or personal property and take the best deal, which is often not even a good deal. The difference between what you should or could have gotten and what you had to take is a nonquantifiable cost. Now, if you had opted out of the government will and could therefore set a more reasonable timeframe for the sale, your beneficiaries would probably get more for your assets. In addition, when the beneficiaries sell the assets themselves—rather than through the court— they are in a much better bargaining position, as potential buyers don't necessarily know that they are desperate.

While this is true of any personal property, it is especially so of real estate. Unless the potential buyer is specifically notified that the house must be sold, he or she won't know what your position is. The sale certainly won't attract those savvy real estate investors that a court auction would.

There are also unquantifiable costs if the estate contains a business. Most businesses, in order to remain solvent, require the ability to make snap decisions. That will not happen once the business falls into the government's hands. A business is like any other asset—it must go through the probate process, which is often fraught with delays. You know the saying "time is money"? Well, every minute that your business is tied up in probate, it could be losing value, and this money is coming out of your beneficiaries' pockets.

Again, when selling real estate through probate (at least in California), you're required to file special forms with the court. One of the main provisions of this special contract is that you must notify the buyer that any sale is subject to court confirmation. This is so even if you were lucky enough to be named independent administrator executor. Remember earlier in this chapter that we discussed the Independent Administration of Estates Act. Under that law, the executor can take care of estate business without the court's permission, including the sale of estate property; however, real estate is an exception.

When you enter into the contract of sale for the real estate in probate, you must provide notice to the beneficiaries as to the terms of the sale. This is done through what's called a "notice of proposed action to sell real estate." The beneficiaries then have the right to contest or object to the sale. This objection could be based on a number different reasons, including, as we said above, that they don't believe the sales price is sufficient. Another common reason is that they didn't want the home sold in the first place. This is often the case when a family residence is involved. Or, to put it bluntly, they are just being jerks. Remember that when you use the government will, you don't have the power to choose your beneficiaries—they are chosen according to the intestacy laws. This means those handling the estate are often at the mercy of crazy beneficiaries. I wish this weren't the case, but it is.

The important takeaway here is that whenever you have to put a condition on a contract, you are not going to get top dollar for the real estate. This is because of those savvy buyers we mentioned above. Potential buyers know they might be outbid at auction, and this factors into the price. It makes sense; these buyers put a lot of time into getting contracts for land and getting the funds prepared, all the while risking being outbid in open court by another investor.

PENALTIES AND INTEREST

There are many other unforeseen costs that eat away at the estate, mainly because of the bureaucratic delays inherent in the government will. I have seen it time and time again: the interest on credit card bills, IRS tax debt, and any other obligations continue to grow. When an estate goes into probate, it takes about sixty days before whoever's in charge is fully empowered to act on the estate's behalf. Oftentimes we treat this is as a gray area and still handle matters for the decedent, but that can also cause problems. If the executor makes payments on behalf of the estate and it is later found that he or she shouldn't have made those payments, that individual could be *personally* liable to the estate or its beneficiaries. It's because of this personal liability that we advise responsible parties not to begin making any payments or doing anything until they officially have the power to do so. Unfortunately, the estate's debts continue to mount in the interim.

However, when you opt out of the government will and have an attorney draw up estate planning documents, you grant the person responsible for your estate explicit powers that allow him or her to make payments immediately after your death. This means no delays, no interest and penalties, and, ultimately, more money in your beneficiaries' pockets.

So, as we've seen here, the government will may technically be free for you, but it costs your beneficiaries plenty. The worst part is these are avoidable and unnecessary expenses. We have all been annoyed when, upon opening a credit card bill, we realize how much of our monthly payment is going to the interest; now imagine that eating away at the money that should be going to your children.

In the next chapter, we'll talk about how much time it takes to settle your estate and how delays inherent in the government will can affect your beneficiaries.

CHAPTER 5

Is the Government Will Too Slow?

This is pretty much a rhetorical question. I mean, let's face it—"speed" is not a word most people associate with the government. In fact, it is infamous for its slow-moving bureaucracy in most areas, and the settling of estates is a prime example.

So how can you determine how long the probate will last? Attorneys don't have a crystal ball; they simply estimate the length of time based on the complexity of the estate. One must consider the sophistication of the executor/administrator, the number of beneficiaries, the location of those beneficiaries, and the nature of the assets, including whether the property must be sold, whether there are any unique or collectible assets, whether there is a closely held or family business, and whether there are assets in multiple states or countries. There might also be questions about the title to assets, liens on assets, or litigation concerning the assets or the decedent's manner of death (e.g., car accident). Finally, one must take into account any estate taxes owed, previous income tax or payroll tax liabilities owed by the decedent, or insolvency of the estate.

That said, the least amount of time in which a probate can be completed is six months. It takes a month just to get a court date to open the probate then, under the law, the estate's creditors have four months to come forward and collect their money. Once that time period has expired, you then have to wait another month for the court date to close the probate. Before you know it, six months have passed. And, remember, that is a purely vanilla probate; if there are any problems, it can literally go on forever—or pretty close to it. It is rumored that a house in Orange County has been in an open probate for eighty-five years!

The government will has certain timeframes built into it, which are required by the probate code. No one—not even attorneys or judges—has the power to circumvent these timeframes. The only way to completely avoid them is to avoid probate altogether. We'll talk more later about how you can do this.

ANCILLARY PROBATES

Earlier, I explained how ancillary probates can cost the estate thousands in extraordinary attorney's fees. Well, they also cost the estate a lot of time. In California, any ancillary probates must be resolved before we can close the probate. This means that you have to conduct the probate proceedings in every other state where estate property is located before you can subdue the one here; this essentially doubles the time it takes to administer the estate. But when you opt out by using a trust or other instrument, a trustee or executor of your choosing can administer properties in several states concurrently. They are empowered to handle things in any order they want, in any manner they want, which saves the estate both time and money.

I currently have a probate that has been open for nearly two years due to the oil and gas interests in Oklahoma and Texas. These interests were only worth about forty thousand dollars, but the back and forth with the courts and attorneys in other states has already cost the estate well over $5,000 in additional extraordinary fees. And that's just to transfer the interests. This all could have been avoided if the decedent had engaged in some simple estate planning.

There are other things that can further complicate and delay the completion of the probate process. For example, what if you have to undertake some complex actions during

the probate process? What if you have to go through litigation? What if you have to sell assets in order to raise some
cash? What if there is some dispute over the legitimacy of
the documents? All of these things will increase the time it
takes to close the probate. Fortunately, there are alternatives,
such as a revocable trust, that can kick the government will
to curb. We'll discuss these alternatives in the next chapter.

CHAPTER 6

How to Disinherit the Government

We've been talking a lot about the difference between the government will and drafting your own. Remember, though, from chapter four that even when you have a private will, many of your assets will still have to go through probate. However, there are other tools you can use to plan your estate. In this chapter, we will cover wills in more detail; we will also discuss ways in which you can completely disinherit the government. Trusts are excellent instruments that can express your wishes even more clearly than a will; in fact, they can even help you avoid probate altogether (at least this is the case in California; other states still require probate even if you have a trust, so check your local laws).

Essentially, a trust creates a relationship among three people or entities. There is the "settlor" (the person creating the trust), the "trustee" (the person or entity that holds the property in trust), and the "beneficiary" (the person for whom the property is held). We will discuss the different types of trusts later, but they all have benefits, most notably the ease with which they are administered. As we have said earlier, the faster the estate is administered, the less money must be paid in fees to the court. And, yes, you will have to pay an attorney to create a trust for you, but that trust will save your estate money in the long run. Remember, trusts allow you to avoid probate altogether (in California).

WILLS

A will is the most basic document that will opt you out of the government will, at least to a certain degree. But while it can save you significant fees (provided you include certain provisions such as the waiver of surety bond), it does *not* eliminate all probate fees. That's why, for many people, a will is only part of an optimal estate plan. Still, a private will has many benefits, most notably the ability to leave property to anybody you'd like.

The first thing most people do when drafting a will is decide who will be responsible for administering their estates after they die. This is a very important decision because, no matter how you slice it, being the personal representative of an estate (also known as an executor) is a big job. One does not have to have any special legal or financial skills in order to be an executor; however, one does have to be diligent and completely aboveboard in the handling of the estate. Here are some of the things executors are expected to do.

In a nutshell, the executor's job is to protect the decedent's property for any creditors as well as any beneficiaries. This includes making sure all the estate's debts and taxes have been paid and that the beneficiaries get what's left. The executor must also make major decisions, such as whether to sell real estate or other property.

The first thing the executor does is figure out if the estate has to go through probate; even if it doesn't, the executor still usually has to file the will with the local probate court (which costs fifty dollars in my local county—I'm telling you there are fees everywhere!). They must also notify any interested parties of the decedent's death; this includes credit card companies, banks, and government agencies like Medicare, Social Security, and even the post office. Believe it or not, they also have to notify the Department of Corrections if a beneficiary is currently in a jail or prison. You can't make this stuff up!

The executors also pay the estate's expenses and taxes out of estate assets (this may be the determining factor in whether the executor decides to sell the real estate) and notify creditors of any probate proceedings. They also collect money owed to the estate and set up a bank account for this purpose. Only after the executor has paid all creditors as is necessary can he or she finally oversee the distribution of the remaining estate to the beneficiaries.

When people are making their wills, they can choose anyone they want as their executor; they can even list successive executors, should their first choice be unable or unwilling to act (in fact, this is advisable). Many people choose their oldest children; others choose other relatives or trusted friends to act as executor. The point is that it is their choice.

If you die without a will, the probate court chooses the executor for you. Usually the spouse is given the highest priority. If you do not have a spouse, the court will next look to your parents; if they have predeceased you or cannot serve, your children will then get priority. The court will *not* choose among your children, though; they must decide among themselves who should be the executor. If they cannot agree then it's off to court to ask the judge who the executor will be, and the only people winning are the attorneys (remember that every moment spent in court is costing the estate money). So if, for example, you already know that your surviving parent is not up to the job or that your son and daughter would fight over it, it is imperative that you make your own will. That way, you can prevent future squabbling and choose the person you trust most to take care of your estate. A court is unaware of, nor is it interested in, your family relationships; it will just go down the list and pick someone.

This is especially important if your executor of choice lives outside the United States. The government will specifically excludes foreign persons (including American citizens living in other countries) from serving as executor. That means if your most trusted relative, friend, or confidant lives in Canada, Mexico, or anywhere else outside the United States, that person won't be able to manage your estate unless you specifically elect him or her to do so.

If you do name a foreign person in your will, that individual may have to go through a few extra hoops in order to serve as executor. I've had the "trust versus convenience" debate with many clients over the years, and while convenience is important for some people, most prefer to have someone they trust, no matter where that person lives, manage their estates. On the other hand, the foreign person can decline the job, so you might also want to designate a successor to serve as executor in his or her place.

Children and Guardians

When young people come to my office to discuss making a will, they often begin by asking whether a will is even necessary, given the fact that they don't have many assets. If they are parents, I ask them one of my favorite trick questions:

"What is your most valuable asset?" After pondering this for a few moments, they usually say that their most valuable asset is their 401(k), their vehicles, or perhaps their homes. I then politely point out that their most valuable asset is not any of those things; it is their children. At this point, they are usually feeling pretty guilty and therefore open to what I'm about to tell them next.

I do not say this to make them feel bad; I say it to point out the most glaring omission of the government will: it makes no provisions for the care of the children. So while their monetary assets may be minimal, they have family wealth that must be protected. In their private wills, they'll be able to name a guardian for their minor children. This brings the parents peace of mind, knowing that in the event of their untimely deaths, the guardian *of their choosing* will be responsible—financially and otherwise—for the kids. The fact that the government will leaves that out is unacceptable.

In fact, there is no family code section that provides an order of preference when both parents are deceased. The closest section on point is Family Code Section 3040, which provides that "custody should be granted in the following order of preference according to the best interest of the child as provided in Sections 3011 and 3020." However, this assumes that either both parents are alive or a single parent is alive. However, if neither parent is alive, the court will still look to the best interests of the child. Family Code Sections

3040(a)(2) and (3) offer some guidance. These sections state: "(2) If to neither parent, to the person or persons in whose home the child has been living in a wholesome and stable environment" and then "(3) To any other person or persons deemed by the court to be suitable and able to provide adequate and proper care and guidance for the child." Family Code Section 3040(a)(3) is probably most instructive, and this is where nominations in an estate plan are critical—they remove all of this uncertainty and potential for interpretation.

Many of my clients name multiple successor guardians in case their first choice predeceases them or is otherwise unable to care for the children. Let's say, for example, that you want to name your brother and sister-in-law, a happily married couple, as guardians of your child. And let's say that after your untimely death, they wind up divorcing. Which parent gets your children? Do you want your children to be pawns in someone's divorce? You must prepare for these kinds of events when drafting the will, even if they seem highly unlikely. The bottom line is you want to make sure that your children will be taken care of, and that means preparing for *any* contingency.

In this case, you would state that you want your brother and sister-in-law to be the guardians, but in the event of their divorce, the court must ensure that your child remains in your family (i.e., with your brother). Most people want this clearly spelled out so that the court has no doubt as to their wishes. That way, they know their children won't be caught up in divorce proceedings and potentially a custody battle.

Holographic Wills

We have been discussing ways you can disinherit the government. But what if you want to avoid attorney's fees as well? The simplest and least expensive way to do this is to create a holographic—or handwritten—will. These wills are recognized in most states, including California, and the requirements are generally less stringent than other kinds of wills. However, if these requirements are not met, then the will cannot be validated and you're right back at square one: the estate is probated as if you died with no will at all.

A holographic will must be handwritten and signed by the testator (the person making the will). It does not have to be witnessed or dated, although it's advisable to do both. The date is especially important if you've made more than one will in your lifetime, as you want everyone to know which is your *last* will and testament.

The problem is that most people are not aware of other details that bring their intentions into question. For example, you bequeath your car to "my friend Jane" and you have more than one friend with that name, or you leave money to "my favorite uncle" and you have more than one uncle. That's when fighting begins, and your heirs are left dealing with the consequences of your poorly drafted document. Other people fail to include the entire estate in their holographic wills either because they forgot or because they acquired the property after the will was made and they did not update it. This may result in that property being distributed under intestacy laws—the government will!

TRUSTS

The Basics

In California, the most common and thorough way to ditch the government will is through the use of a revocable living trust. It is also the most cost-efficient. You might be saying, "Okay, but I have to pay an attorney to create the trust, right?" Yes, you do, but in the end you will be saving the estate money in probate fees, which means your kids save money. Take this example: an attorney will charge you between $800 and $1,500 to create the average trust. Now compare this to the current rates in California for probating a $500,000 estate, which is approximately $15,000 in attorney fees and court costs.

As we will see, trusts not only save money; they have several other benefits as well.

Helpful During Life and After Death

Trusts avoid probate fees when someone dies. Arguably this is their main purpose. But most people don't realize trusts can be very valuable during life as well. If you as the settlor are alive but incapacitated (e.g., Alzheimer's, dementia, or an accident), your successor trustee can step in and access your assets, which are now trust assets, to pay for your care. This could mean selling or renting your real estate to pay for assisted living or taking cash distributions from your brokerage account to pay for a nursing home. There are plenty of examples, but remember: a trust may make a world of difference while you're alive as well as when you pass away. A trust truly offers the most flexibility when it comes to unforeseen circumstances.

Simplify Life for the Surviving Spouse

Many trusts are marital trusts; that is they are for the benefits of two spouses. When one spouse dies, a trust has specific provisions to deal with this occurrence. Let's face it:

both spouses rarely die at the same time. A trust is designed to minimize the disruption in the surviving spouse's life; it will alleviate a ton of stress and even help with the grieving process. The last thing widows or widowers need is to be running off to court and paying attorneys so they can access their own assets after their spouses die.

Private Administration

A trust guarantees that your estate will be administered privately. In California, all probate cases are a matter of public record; this means that just about any person can go down to the country courthouse, hand the clerk a few bucks, and make copies of any probate proceeding being handled in that county.

This includes a peek at the decedent's will, as well as the person's assets and debts. If you think *that's* invasive, remember that the accounting of the estate is also there for prying eyes to see. This is a very detailed record of all the money received and spent in an estate; it includes everything, from how much was spent on diapers and other items to major purchases. It might also include things that perhaps the decedent didn't want people to know were purchased. The only way to avoid this is to opt out of probate with a living trust.

Informal and Swift

We discussed earlier how the government will moves along at a snail's pace. Trusts, on the other hand, are a study in speed and efficiency. Remember how we discussed how long ancillary probates can take? Well, a trust allows for multistate administrations to occur simultaneously, saving your estate time and money.

The reason trusts move so quickly is that they are not subject to the rules of the probate court. Let's return to the topic of real estate for a moment. Remember that the probate court requires notification for the sale of real estate; in California, that notice must be at least fifteen days. This can be problematic. I recently had a probate case that involved the sale of real estate. We found a buyer, but before we could close on the sale, we had to make sure we had given the beneficiaries fifteen days' notice. Fortunately for the estate, the buyer was willing to agree to a longer escrow; however, this is not a chance you want to take. Recall the earlier discussion about unseen costs of the government will? Well, had this buyer walked away, I would have had to look for another buyer (and charged extraordinary fees to do so). In addition, the next buyer may have made a much lower offer, which would have also cost the estate money.

Trusts are also very informal, which is a huge plus for beneficiaries. Most people don't realize that funds cannot be distributed from a probate until the very end of the probate proceedings. Once I inform them of this, they are even more eager to avoid court through the use of a trust.

This is especially true if your beneficiaries are counting on your money after you pass. Perhaps your kids have to pay their college tuition, or some other expense arises. The bottom line is that everyone needs cash to live, so why not ensure that your loved ones get it as quickly as possible? Compare this to predatory inheritance-funding companies that loan money as advances to beneficiaries and charge 30 percent premiums for doing so. With the government will, this is the only way to get cash quick.

Trusts move quickly. There is an administration process; however, in certain circumstances, the trustee has the discretion to make a distribution before the end of that process. This discretion can be a lifesaver if one of the beneficiaries truly needs the money right away.

I had a client whose mother had recently passed away. The mother had set up an $800,000 trust, of which my client was both the trustee and a beneficiary. The administration progressed smoothly for a few weeks then I got the call. My client's son—who was the other beneficiary of the trust— needed money right away due to some tragedy. He would eventually receive about half of his grandmother's trust, but my client wanted to know whether we could get him some money before the estate administration was complete. The first step was for me to look at how the trust was structured and what kind of assets it contained; this way, I'd be able to determine the condition of the estate and whether we could do what's called an "advance distribution." Depending on how a trust was set up, the trustee sometimes has the power to make a distribution at any time. Of course, the trustee can later be held liable for actions not taken in the best interest of the trust. But that's what having an attorney is all about; we help you make these decisions and try to keep you out of trouble.

In this case, I was able to tell my client that, based on the composition of the estate (i.e., that we had cash and very little debt), her son could get his distribution ahead of time. Greatly relieved, she asked a few more questions, and when we got off the phone, she felt comfortable writing her son a check for $30,000. Tragedy averted.

Clearly, this story had a happy ending. Now let's take a look at what would have happened if my client's mother had the government will. Well, first of all, we would have had to file a petition asking the court to allow us to distribute the funds early. This is available in most state courts, but the judges first have to rule on whether it is truly an emergency. In this situation, my client's emergency was not really an emergency (her son needed a new car), so we don't know whether the judge would have allowed an advance distribution or not. Assuming the judge did allow it, we would then have had to file an accounting with the court to prove that it is a liquid estate and that the debts do not exceed the assets. This is because the judge cannot let money be distributed until he or she is certain that all the creditors of the estate will be satisfied. Regardless of the outcome, we would have had to spend money on the petition. Thanks to the trust, I was able to do a quick accounting and make a short phone call from my office, saving my client money and headaches.

Trusts Are Thorough

Many people don't know this, but trusts are typically much more thorough documents than wills. This is because the settlor of a trust can include very specific provisions that span multiple years. That's not to say that a carefully crafted will could not accomplish the same things, but trusts make it much simpler.

Let's say your children are your beneficiaries, and they are not very proficient with money. In fact, they are what we call spendthrifts, or people who spend irresponsibly. You can use a trust to restrict the manner in which the beneficiaries receive their money. You can instruct the trustee to distribute the money when they reach certain ages, or you might decide that they should never get the money outright and instead provide them with a monthly income for life or over a certain period. In doing so, you substitute your judgment for theirs, and you just might protect your children from their inheritance.

You might be thinking, *Did he just say "protect my children* from *their inheritance"?* Yes, that's exactly what I said. In theory, it sounds like a great idea to give your children their entire inheritance at once, but in reality it may not be what's best for them. Let's say you don't place restrictions on how your children receive the money—they get it all upon your death and can use it in any way they wish. This is fine if they are mature adults, but what if they are only eighteen or even nineteen when you pass away? I don't know about you, but when I was eighteen, receiving a large influx of cash or property would not have been very good for me. I often tell my clients that a large inheritance plus an eighteen-year-old beneficiary equals a Ferrari and a drug problem. I say this jokingly, but it may not be far from the truth.

It is also not an uncommon problem. Many people who come into my office for estate planning are concerned with protecting their children...from themselves. Perhaps their kids have made poor financial decisions in the past, or—as is often the case—are battling addictions. Now, I know I am stepping on dangerous ground here; it is never easy to advise people to protect assets against the actions of family members. After all, it is parents' natural instinct to give their children everything. However, I always advise my clients to be honest with themselves about their children's abilities to manage their finances. If there are issues in this regard then I move on to the even more difficult conversation: presenting the client with options on how they can restrict their children's access to the assets when they (the parents) pass away.

I had a client who passed away from cancer. His son had a severe drug addiction; in fact, he is currently in prison for actions relating to that addiction. My client was well aware of the problem, and, unlike many parents, he was willing to take the steps to deal with it. He had me create a trust and chose not his son but a loyal friend as trustee. Per the trust terms, this friend was empowered to make distributions only if he felt it was in the son's best interest. It also empowered him to refuse to make distributions to the son while he was in prison, thereby preserving his assets. If and when this young man goes into recovery and shows that he is capable of making responsible decisions, the inheritance from his father will be waiting for him. This is the kind of gift you can leave your at-risk children when you opt out of the government will. If the father had not engaged in estate planning, his son would have received his full inheritance under the laws of intestacy, with no restrictions, and, in all likelihood, would have squandered it on his addiction and maybe even died from it.

The worst situation I've ever seen was a beneficiary with a gambling problem. It sounds strange, but while drugs are terrible, there are only so many you can do in a night. But there is no limit to how much you can lose while gambling. You can wager anywhere from a penny to a million dollars and lose it all in the blink of an eye. It was for this reason that my clients were adamant about restricting their child's access to the money.

As I mentioned above, the trust can also be crafted so that the child *never* has unrestricted use of the money. You can instruct the trustee to give your son or daughter money each month, and you can specify what that money can be used for. While you can specify an amount, I don't advise this, especially if it is a long-term trust. For example, in 1975, you might've thought leaving five hundred dollars a month to your children would be more than enough to keep them happy, but in today's world, five hundred dollars doesn't get you much. Instead, I recommend specifying that the money be distributed for things like health, education, maintenance, and support. We have a case before the court right now where an older gentleman left his family his assets in a poorly drafted trust at the rate of three hundred dollars a month. The trust is going to burn through more in accounting, tax, attorney, and trustee fees than the actual distributions. Probably not what the decedent had in mind.

You can instruct the trustee to make certain purchases or investments, such as an immediate or deferred annuity, on your beneficiaries' behalf. There are many kinds of annuities—some good, some bad—so I always suggest that my clients seek the advice of a registered investment advisor or other investment professional before purchasing one. For example, you can have an annuity that will last for the lifetime of the beneficiary. Or, if the beneficiary is older, you can purchase an annuity that's guaranteed for a certain timeframe (i.e., a number of years); if the beneficiary dies before the end of that period, his or her children receive the difference. The advantage of using an annuity is that it does not require the trust to remain open. If a trust remains open, it continues to generate fees, including, but not limited to, trustee fees (the trustee gets a percentage of the trust amount; it is either specified in the document itself or determined by the court), tax preparation fees, legal fees, and accounting fees.

Annuities are a great way to restrict your child's use of the inheritance and save fees associated with a trust; however, there are also risks you should be aware of. For example, your child could decide to sell his or her annuity or income stream to a third party or back to the annuity company itself. The company would pay a lump sum, out of which they take a hefty fee. This loophole allows your beneficiary to defeat your intent and possibly lose money in the process.

Irrevocable Trusts

When I am discussing trusts with my clients, they often want to know the difference between revocable and irrevocable trusts. I tell them that the names are self-explanatory.

An irrevocable trust is one that, once created and funded, cannot be changed. On the other hand, a revocable trust is one in which the settlor reserves the power to either change the terms or terminate the trust completely. Not surprisingly, revocable trusts are much more common, as people want to reserve the right to make changes as they get older, whether it's to add or remove assets or to whom they leave those assets when they die. In fact, 95 percent of trusts we create are revocable.

Irrevocable trusts are valuable, though; they can be used for tax reasons or asset protection. In most cases, the assets are not considered owned by the settlor; therefore, they are not counted as part of that person's wealth when assessing whether he or she is eligible for college financing, government benefits, or other assistance. They are also often not subject to a person's creditors; that means the creditor cannot attach the trust property to satisfy a debt.

In contrast, the settlors of a revocable trust retain so much control that state and federal governments don't even recognize it as a separate entity. For example, most revocable trusts don't require a separate federal tax return; they are reported on the individual tax returns like they didn't exist. Despite this lack of protection, most people still prefer the revocable trust because of its ease of use.

It's worth noting that trusts are not very lucrative for attorneys. Sure, they get the fee for creating the trust, but they make little money when the decedent passes. Given the high probate fees, it makes more sense, from a business perspective, to discourage trusts. That said, any ethical attorney will discuss all your options with you and if a trust makes sense, draw one up. I've heard stories of attorneys many years ago talking clients out of trusts just so that they could probate the estates and collect the higher fees. These were rumors, and I hope they aren't true—perhaps this is where all the bad attorney jokes come from?

Special-Needs Trusts

Some of my most motivated clients are those who want to provide for someone who is elderly, disabled, or otherwise impaired. As we have covered in this book, there are several ways they can do this; however, if the intended beneficiaries are receiving any kind of assistance from the federal and/or state government as a result of their disabilities then there are very specific steps that must be taken in order to protect those benefits.

People over the age of sixty-five who are blind or disabled are entitled to receive regular income from the federal government called supplemental security income (SSI). In this case, "disabled" is defined as having a mental or physical impairment severe enough that the person cannot work; the period of this disability must be no less than twelve months. In addition, in order to receive SSI, one must not exceed a certain amount of income and assets; essentially, the government wants to make sure that it is giving money to those who truly need it. Therefore, this amount is very little ($2,000) but excludes certain assets such as the residence, furniture, clothes, one vehicle, and some other items needed for personal care.

There are also state benefits a person with disabilities might be entitled to (again, please be sure that you check the laws of your particular state). In California, a person collecting SSI is also automatically eligible for Medi-Cal, which is the state version of Medicaid. Other benefits one might receive include housing subsidies (known as "Section 8"), food stamps, and help with utilities such as electric, heat, hot water, etc. However, as I mentioned above, if the recipient receives any income or assets above the permitted amount, these benefits will either be decreased or end entirely. An inheritance, whether through probate, a regular will, or even trusts, can count as income.

Here is a typical scenario: parents of an adult disabled

child come into my office to engage in estate planning. Specifically, they want make sure that the child's needs are provided for after they die. Now, let's say that during the consultation, I learn that their son or daughter is collecting SSI benefits and receiving medical coverage through Medi-Cal. Now, under normal circumstances, I would advise them to opt out of the government will and avoid probate; however, in this case, that wouldn't be enough. If the child gets their full and unrestricted inheritance under a will or via distribution from certain types of trusts, he or she may no longer be able to collect those government benefits. That means that this inheritance must be enough to sustain him or her for life, including housing, food, clothing, transportation, medical expenses, and so on. If not, that person will soon find himself or herself out of money and reapplying for those benefits, which is a terrible waste of money. Furthermore, this can be a long, drawn-out, and difficult bureaucratic process.

People who know about the risk to their child's benefits might consider disinheriting the child altogether; they feel like they can arrange for their other children, or someone else in the family, to promise to take care of the person with special needs. I strongly advise them against this. The relative may have every intention in the world of carrying out their parents' wishes, but the fact of the matter is no one can predict what will happen in the future. What if the sibling gets into financial or legal trouble? Their creditors can take the money intended to help the special-needs person. Or the sibling could pass away, and unless they have made special provisions in their estate plans, the money might go to someone unable—or unwilling—to help.

This is when I tell the parents that their best option is to create a third-party special-needs trust. With this type of trust, the beneficiaries have no control over the assets; they cannot revoke or amend it. Most importantly, the beneficiary is not considered the owner of the trust property, so it cannot be counted as income or assets that will affect SSI, Medi-Cal, or any other government assistance. Instead, the trust owns the assets, and it is in the trustee's sole discretion to make distributions that help the beneficiary with certain expenditures, such as the phone bill, education, or car repairs. The trust is not required to make any cash payments to the beneficiary, as that would count as income and would therefore reduce benefits. Using trust money to buy a home for the beneficiary is fine, but this may reduce government assistance related to the residence. That aside, a third-party special-needs trust is still the best way to protect loved ones with special needs. It is especially critical when they will only be inheriting a small amount of money and therefore in danger of running out of funds. With this trust in place, beneficiaries can continue to live on their government assistance and use the trust money as a safety net or to supplement their quality of life. And since they are not considered the owners of the trust property, they will not have to pay the government back for the assistance they received.

The grantor can set up the trust to take effect either during his or her lifetime or upon his or her death. Many prefer it to take effect during their lives because this allows them to start funding it; it also allows them to revoke or amend it (for example, if the law regarding disability benefits changes). Once the grantor dies, the trust becomes irrevocable and, as I said above, out of the beneficiary's control. If the trust is set up to take effect after the grantor's death then it will be funded per his or her testamentary documents (i.e., a will or trust).

There is another kind of special-needs trust known as a first-party (or litigation) special-needs trust. This is a trust funded by some sort of windfall (such as winning the lottery or a lawsuit, or an inheritance that is not protected by a third-party trust). Normally, such a windfall would count as income and affect government benefits; however, when a first-party trust is in place, the special-needs person is able to keep these funds and his or her government assistance. This kind of trust must be created by a parent, grandparent, or guardian of the special-needs person; in some cases, it is created by the probate court. Now, let's say in the example above that the beneficiary was injured in a car accident, which resulted in his or her disability. Unable to work, he or she started collecting SSI and Medi-Cal benefits. He or she has also initiated a lawsuit against the person responsible for the car accident. There is a great likelihood that he or she will win the suit; the problem is that any award received will reduce the person's benefits or disqualify him or her altogether. So his or her parents set up a first-party trust. When the lawsuit is over, the winnings fund the trust and are not counted as income. While this is not estate planning per se, it is another way for parents or grandparents to make sure the special-needs person is taken care of.

It is important to note that these trusts are not a way to hide large amounts of money so someone can also receive government assistance. Rather, they are for people who really need the assistance and will use the trust as a supplementary income to help them live a better quality of life.

Are you feeling better yet? Like you have more options to protect your assets—and your loved ones—from the government? Well, you're going to feel even better when we get to the next chapter!

CHAPTER 7

Other Documents
That Help You Opt Out

Wills and trusts are the primary ways to opt out of the government will, but they are not the only ones. In this chapter, we will explore some of the other instruments you can use to avoid probate and protect your assets.

Joint Tenancy

So let's say you have a very straightforward and simple estate, but it's still high enough in value that you want to avoid probate. In this case, many people choose to put their property in joint tenancy. Others already have their property in joint tenancy, yet they have no idea what that really means.

When two people take title to property as joint tenants, they have created what's called a right of survivorship.

Basically, it's the last man standing—whoever survives the other takes full title of the property. Officially, the title is written as "A and B as joint tenants with right of survivorship." However, according to the California civil code, all you really have to do is take title, joint tenancy, and—voila!—you have an implied right of survivorship. It's one of the simplest things you can do to protect your assets.

Say, for example, you take title to your house as joint tenants with your brother. When you die, your half of the house will automatically go to him. The house will not be included in the probate; however, an affidavit of death of joint tenant must be filed with the county in which the property is located. This document states that the house will be retitled in the surviving tenant's name alone. The same goes if you want to leave the house to your son or daughter. You just title the house as joint tenants with your child, and when you die, he or she will get your house without having to go through probate. Sounds good, right?

Even better, you don't need any documents to set up a joint tenancy, and there is virtually no cost for taking title as joint tenants. There is a cost for the surviving tenant to receive the property, but it is a minimal one. The affidavit of death of joint tenant used in California can be prepared by a layperson or by an attorney for a relatively small fee. A legal document preparer, or even the country clerk, can also help.

Now that we've heard why joint tenancy is good, let's get

to the downside. Joint tenancy is what I refer to as reckless title. In other words, you don't know who will be the first to die, so you have no idea who will end up with the property. Not very good planning, and the next question becomes: what will happen when the surviving tenant passes away?

Once the first tenant dies (assuming two joint tenants), the joint tenancy is dissolved; this means the property will be subject to probate unless the surviving tenant does something to protect it. To do this, the person can create a trust, which will avoid probate entirely, or he or she can create a will, which, as we have seen, is not quite as good but is better than doing nothing. The problem is it may not even be possible for the surviving tenant to do either of these things.

Let's say a husband and wife take title to real estate as joint tenants. They go on to share a long, wonderful life together until one dies at the ripe old age of ninety-five. It is very possible that the surviving spouse (and joint tenant) will be unable to put that property into a trust. He or she may be legally incapacitated due to dementia or some other defect of the mind. In that case, the heirs are stuck watching the train wreck because when their second parent dies, the property will go through probate.

There are also issues that come up when you hold real estate with a party other than your spouse. What these issues are depends on the situation. For instance, if you hold the property with your child as joint tenants, you can have an informal arrangement that allows you to live in the home for the rest of your life. But what about third parties? Remember that whomever you hold tenancy with has equal ownership of the house and has equal control over the property.

This brings us to yet another potential problem. A property held in joint tenancy is considered an asset for the purposes of creditors. If there is a judgment against your child for failure to pay a credit card debt or student loan or if they are sued in a wrongful death action or a defunct business deal, your property can be taken to satisfy the debt. We'll get into this in more detail when we cover making gifts to your children.

Transfer-on-Death—Pay-on-Death

Another method used to avoid probate is the "pay-on-death" (POD) or "transfer-on-death" (TOD) designation. These are offered by most banks and other financial institutions such as brokerage houses. You simply notify the institution that holds your accounts that you want to add a transfer-on-death or pay-on-death designation to each account. You then add the specific people you want to get your assets when you die. You don't need to create any other legal documents or pay an attorney. It's really that simple!

Like joint tenancy, pay-on-death and transfer-on-death

accounts also have their drawbacks. The first would be similar to that of using joint tenancy. Remember the example of the ninety-five-year-old couple? Well, if your pay-on-death designation is your spouse, he or she may not have the mental capacity to transfer those assets into a trust once he or she receives them after you die. If this is the case, the assets will end up in probate when that person dies, and the beneficiaries will be back at square one. That's the square where you waste a bunch of money and attorneys get rich.

I usually advise clients to use TOD and POD account designations when they have only one or two accounts; otherwise, it gets too complicated. Say you want to change beneficiaries or add new ones—for example, when a grandchild is born or one of your children passes away. If you have TOD and POD designations on your accounts, you have to change each individual account at each institution. On the other hand, if you have a trust document controlling the general disposition of your assets, you only have to make one change, and that's to the trust itself. You also have much more flexibility and control when using a trust than with a POD or a TOD designation.

Another drawback to using these designations is when a beneficiary dies before you. TOD and POD designations do not account for this situation—if the named beneficiary is already dead when you pass away, the funds go to the next beneficiary in line (this person is called the "contingent beneficiary"). But what happens when the final contingent beneficiary dies before you? Then the account must go through probate or possibly to someone else based on the terms of the POD contract you signed with the bank. However, when you set up a trust, you not only have contingent beneficiaries, but you can also account for several lines of family members. In some cases, these lines can be nearly infinite, leaving little or no chance of probate. This is one of the things wealthy people do to preserve their money for future generations. I'll talk about that in greater detail in the next chapter.

I also recommend the use of a POD or TOD designation when clients have a single checking account that they use to pay bills. Typically, they put their children on this account, at least as authorized signers. Many senior citizens don't enjoy the idea of paying bills (I can't blame them; I hate doing it too), so their children step in to help. Since most banks will not let you add an authorized signer to a living trust account (probably for liability reasons), I recommend that we use the trust for the majority of their assets and use a TOD designation for that one small checking account. Every month or so, my client as trustee will transfer funds into the checking account, thus allowing the child to write checks on his or her behalf. It's really the best of both worlds as long as you don't keep a lot of money in the account.

The Hazards of Gifting to Children

Many people ask me about gifting their assets to their children while they are still alive. That way, they don't have to deal with wills or trusts because they're essentially leaving themselves penniless. Inherent in this sort of agreement is that the children allow their parents to continue using these assets while they're still alive. Some parents choose a combination of these methods: they gift their residence to their children and put POD designations on their bank accounts. In limited circumstances, this can be effective because it saves attorney's fees and avoids probate at the same time. However, this kind of arrangement also carries a lot of risk. Let's take a look at why.

When you gift your property to children but still want to retain control, your children become the official owners, and they are (generously) letting you use it. Now, I know what you're thinking: *These are my children; they would never kick me out.* And you may very well be right. Still, I often am hesitant to recommend this option to my clients. No matter how well they think they know their children, anything can happen. My only responsibility is to protect my client.

There is another huge risk in titling your assets to your children, and it's one we've touched on before. Once those assets are in their names, they become subject to your children's creditors and estate plans.

If your child incurs a liability, such as a car accident with a death or catastrophic injury, any assets in his or her name may be used to satisfy those debts. What if your child has a business deal that goes bad? What if your child gets into credit card, student, or car debt? And if your son or daughter thinks he or she can get out of it by declaring bankruptcy, he or she is sorely mistaken. The bankruptcy court will take control of your assets to satisfy the creditors—remember, as far as the world knows, these things do not belong to you; they belong to your children.

Or what happens if, God forbid, your child predeceases you? Because the asset is in your child's name, it will be distributed according to his or her estate plan. Hopefully he or she *doesn't* have the government will because if he or she does, you may have to start paying rent to someone else. The probate court requires it. But let's say they did opt out, and now your property goes to your grandchildren. Are they as nice as your kids? Do you even get along with them? What happens if the property goes to your daughter-in-law or son-in-law? Did they always hate you and now that their spouse is gone, they can't wait to kick you out of the house? Perhaps you think you know the answers to these questions, but are you willing to bet your house and security on it?

In my experience, most families are cordial, but I have also witnessed cases where someone dies and the veneer of civility dies along with them. The easy money of an inheritance can make people do things they normally wouldn't. Don't be the victim.

There are a host of other, more subtle reasons why putting your children's names on your real estate is a poor way to engage in estate planning. One of these reasons is taxes. Let's say you put your house in your children's names then later decide to sell that house, whether because you are moving into assisted living or simply want to downsize. If you do, you will find that Section 121 of the Internal Revenue Code—the section that handles the taxability of the sale of a personal residence—no longer applies to you. Under this section, you currently get to exclude $500,000 in capital gains if you're married, or $250,000 if you're single, from the sale of your personal residence that you lived in for two of the last five years. But if you've put your kids' names on the title, you no longer get this exemption because you no longer own the residence; they do. Furthermore, since your children own the house but don't live there, it is technically a rental property. That means there is no exemption; you are paying full gains on the property, and your children will likely have rental income.

Assume for a moment that you bought your house twenty years ago for $100,000. A few years ago, you began thinking about estate planning, but instead of going to an attorney, you took your hairdresser's or bartender's advice and put the house in your kids' names. Think it sounds crazy that somebody took this kind of advice from a hair-dresser or bartender? Well, I hear about it all the time! Now you decide that it is time for you and your wife to move into an assisted care facility so you can lead a more carefree lifestyle. You are thrilled when you learn the house has been appraised at $600,000. And when you call your children and tell them of your decision, they are completely supportive. I guess you raised them right!

You sell your house for $600,000 and decide that you have plenty of money to live in your assisted care facility for as long as you need to. Life is looking pretty good. Then April rolls around, and it's time to see the tax guy. You tell him all about the sale of the home and how wonderful the assisted facility is.

It's all going great until you hand your tax guy the document showing the sale of your house. If he's reputable, he takes one look, sees that it lists your children as the owners, and asks what that's all about, to which you reply that your hairdresser or bartender gave you great advice on how to avoid paying an estate planner a few thousand dollars to draw up a trust. You probably throw in a few choice words about what a rip-off attorneys are. Don't worry; I've heard them all.

This is the moment when the penny wise find out that they've been pound foolish. Basically, your tax guy is about to look at you pityingly and say that, unfortunately, you have a large tax bill on the sale of your home. "Whoa, whoa, whoa!" you say. "I looked this up on the Internet"—where most people get their tax information. "The gain on the house was only five hundred thousand dollars, so according to Internal Revenue Code Section 121, and since it was my personal residence, I get to exclude it." And you would be right, had you still been the owner of the house. The problem is that although you lived there at the time of the sale, you had already gifted it to your children. Therefore, the $500,000 of gain is going to cost you $100,000 or more in taxes. Looks like the few thousand dollars you saved by not hiring an attorney didn't pay off after all. Like I said, penny wise, pound foolish.

Life Insurance Policies and Annuities

These are other ways you can avoid the government will; some of them, like trusts, can help you avoid probate altogether. Still, you should be leery whenever someone suggests using life insurance or annuities in this manner. As I am not a financial advisor, I always recommend that my clients speak to one before proceeding.

There are many different types of annuities, but they are generally defined as a financial product sold by financial institutions (such as a bank or life insurance company).

The institution accepts funds from an individual or another institution; it then grows these funds and makes regular payments to the "annuitant" (beneficiary) later on. Perhaps you've seen those commercials about people receiving an annuity after they've won a judgment in a lawsuit. This is a very common form of annuity, but for our purposes here, annuity refers to a retirement or estate planning tool. When structured correctly, annuities can help you avoid probate while guaranteeing yourself a lifetime income. Upon your death, any money left on the policy will automatically go to your children. Not all policies have a death benefit, however, so check with your financial advisor and ask a lot of questions—be sure it is the right annuity for you.

Life insurance policies are also excellent in this regard. It works like this: you deposit a lump sum with a life insurance company. You can borrow against that amount, and when you die, the value of the policy, as determined by the insurance company, goes to your children without going through probate. In addition, since you are able to borrow against the policy, you don't give up the liquidity while you are alive. Typically, life insurance policies are used for investment purposes, so, again, I highly recommend that you seek the advice of a financial advisor *and* your attorney before using it as a probate avoidance vehicle.

As you can see, there are several documents (other than a will) that can protect your financial assets. However, as important as your money is, there are other things—like your health—that are far more important. In this next chapter, we'll discuss how a failure to engage in estate planning can affect your physical and mental wellbeing. In fact, it can literally make you sick.

CHAPTER 8

Other Essential Testamentary Documents

So far, we've spent a lot of time discussing the ways you can use wills and trusts to disinherit the government, and even avoid probate altogether, after your death. But what if you become ill or have an accident that does not kill you but leaves you unable to manage your affairs while still alive? I always advise my clients to prepare for this possibility as well as the eventuality of death. It is my opinion that any comprehensive estate plan must include two documents in addition to the trust: a power of attorney (POA) and an advanced health care directive (AHCD).

Power of Attorney

A power of attorney allows you to name an agent who will take control of your finances should you become incapacitated (alive but unable to make decisions). In essence, that person becomes your mouthpiece when you cannot speak for yourself. The POA empowers your agent to access any accounts that are not held in trust, including custodial accounts such as IRAs, 401(k)s, and life insurance policies, as well as real estate (again, as long as it's not held in trust).

Think of a POA as a complement to your other estate planning documents. When a trust is in place, the trustee will be able to handle trust assets on your behalf; however, he or she will not be able to handle the custodial accounts mentioned above or perhaps any real estate that was erroneously left out of the trust.

Let's just say, for example, that you were in a serious car accident and have slipped into a coma. Your personal assets are not enough to provide for your medical care, and your family will have to dip into your custodial accounts, such as your IRA, to pay for it. Even if you have a trust, your IRA company will not listen to the successor trustee, nor will they listen to the executor of your will because you are not deceased. The only person they will listen to is the agent you designated on a power-of-attorney form. This may be your wife, your child, or a trusted friend. But the bottom line is if you don't have a power of attorney, your IRA, 401(k), or life insurance assets are not available to you, even in an emergency.

The same scenario is applicable if you get dementia or Alzheimer's. Let's say you have lived a long, happy life, but toward the end, you get Alzheimer's. Your children, who love you very much, step in to handle your finances. Part of planning for retirement is calculating how much to take out of your IRA; however, no matter how carefully you planned, a change in circumstances may require that you take out more money. Your children must have power of attorney in order to withdraw these funds for your care.

In addition, a power of attorney can amend or make changes to your revocable living trust during your incapacitation. Take a case where a married couple has created a revocable living trust. If one of them becomes incapacitated and the other wants to amend, he or she may not be able to do this (it depends on the terms of the trust). However, if they also have a power of attorney, the other spouse can make whatever changes he or she desires (unless limited in the actual trust document).

As you can see, the power of attorney is a critical part of estate and retirement planning. And as you can probably surmise by now, the government will contains no such provisions.

Advanced Health Care Directive (AHCD)

Many people I speak to are not quite sure what an AHCD is; they confuse it with a "do not resuscitate" order, a directive to physicians, or some other document hospitals have them fill out before getting a medical procedure. Well, after spending many years looking over these various documents, I can tell you that none of them are as comprehensive as an advanced health care directive.

An AHCD allows you to name an agent to make general medical decisions for you in the event of your incapacitation. This includes medical and mental conditions. Furthermore, this document gives you the opportunity to make your wishes known regarding your health care, should your agent ever need to make a decision on your behalf.

An advanced health-care directive also allows you to designate how you'd like to be disposed of after you die. You can elect to be buried or cremated and, if it's the latter, state where you want your ashes to be spread. It also allows you to authorize an autopsy or prohibits somebody from performing an autopsy if are uncomfortable with it. You can elect to be an organ donor through your AHCD, or if you don't want to make these decisions right now, you can simply empower your agent to make them when the time comes. But the bottom line is these decisions cannot be made unless you authorize your agent to do so.

Most of what we have been discussing in this book deals with financial assets, but the AHCD deals with the most important asset of all: your health and well-being. To most of us, that is even more important than saving money or taxes. The AHCD will allow your doctors and health-care facilities to avoid delay by having your agent authorize necessary care for you. Delays can be very costly in health care, both to your health and your wallet, and AHCDs help to avoid those delays and expedite decision making on your behalf.

A crudely named yet very important part of your advanced health-care directive is the "pull-the-plug provision." This was created in recognition that modern medical science can keep someone alive, sometimes indefinitely, by artificial means. Obviously, this clause is not for someone who has a reasonable hope of recovery but for those who have no brain activity and would die if not for the machines to which he or she is hooked up (feeding tubes and respirators). A pull-the-plug provision instructs your agent to remove those artificial means and allow you to die naturally, usually allowing for pain relief so you are comfortable or at least in minimal pain. This is one of the most important provisions and one nearly all my clients want to include in their estate plans. The reality is that urgent care costs can run up to $100,000 a day, causing crushing debt and even bankruptcy. No one wants to be that kind of burden on his or her family.

In addition to saving money and making your wishes known, this provision also relieves your family of the burden of making a very difficult decision. My clients often misunderstand the purpose of this directive; they believe that it gives their family the power to make this decision. That is incorrect. The provision is an instruction made by *you* while you are in full possession of your faculties to let your loved ones know exactly what *you* want if and when that time comes. By making this *your* decision, you are freeing them from the responsibility (and possible guilt) of having to make the choice for you.

Oftentimes, people try to draft a power of attorney and/ or advanced health-care directive on their own. They find boilerplate documents online and fill them out, thinking they can save the attorney fees. This is when I remind you again: you get what you pay for. When clients bring these documents to me to review, I often find that they are missing some very important provisions. For example, it is advisable that you specifically state on your power of attorney and/or advanced health-care directive that copies of your documents can be relied on by third parties. Why? Because there are a host of situations in which the originals cannot be located. For example, what if you're on vacation when you become incapacitated? It is very possible that health-care providers will receive a fax or e-mail version of your advanced health-care directive, and you certainly don't want your treatment to be delayed because they are only allowed to rely on the original documents. This one omitted provision to your directive can, in the event of an emergency, cause a lot of problems for you and heartache for your loved ones because of delays.

We understand how it can be tempting to avoid those attorney's fees; however, it is often a case again of being penny wise and pound foolish. The important thing to remember is that you are not paying a lawyer simply so he or she can fill out paperwork for you; you are paying for his or her *knowledge* of the law and how it applies to your unique situation. A lawyers training and experience allows him or her to recognize the nuances, whether it is something that is missing from a document or an unwanted provision that was included. What you save in attorney's fees can wind up costing you—or your estate—a lot more money. It can also cause delays in decision-making regarding your assets and health care.

In the next chapter, we'll discuss the effect the government will has on wealthy individuals and how they can protect their assets for generations to come.

CHAPTER 9

How the Government Will Decimates Wealth (and How You Can Protect It)

So far we've been covering standard estate planning principles—namely, what average people can do to protect the assets they've worked so hard for and preserve them for their intended beneficiaries rather than handing them over to the government. Well, the wealthy are just as vulnerable to court and attorney's fees as the rest of us; in fact, the more money you have, the more can be eaten away by the piranhas in the probate system (not to mention the tax code).

Charitable giving is another concern, particularly for the more affluent. Many wealthy people use philanthropy to support causes near and dear to their hearts and do good in the world, and they usually want to make sure the giving continues after they've passed away. For this to happen, however, they have to opt out of the government will. As I've stated before, the government will does not take the decedent's intent into account. This includes any charitable intent. It is simply not a part of the distribution scheme.

On the other hand, you don't have to be wealthy to be a philanthropist. Charitable giving is also a wonderful option for anyone—regardless of his or her financial status—who does not have close relatives to which to leave his or her assets. When I sit down with these clients, I give them my speech about how the government will works then I discuss what might happen if they die without engaging in estate planning. If, at that time, their parents, children, or siblings are not alive to receive their inheritance, any assets will go to whatever blood relations they have, no matter how distant those relations are. I then ask them how they feel about this. Are they close with these people? Do they care if they get all of their hard-earned money, residence, and personal property? Or would they prefer that it go to a charity? Some people really perk up when I suggest this. Perhaps they never felt like they had enough to give, and they like the idea that their money may go to a worthy cause rather than an aunt they never liked (or knew). If charitable giving is important to you then you must opt out of the government will and name these charities with the same specificity that you would name any other beneficiary.

Remember the case of Roman Blum? Although he was savvy enough to amass great wealth, he neglected to protect that wealth with proper estate planning. His money could have benefitted countless people through charitable giving; instead, New York State will soon be $40 million richer. So it doesn't matter whether you are super-wealthy or can barely pay your mortgage; if you don't opt out, your money will never get to the people you want to help. Certainly, no one will benefit but the lawyers and some unknown relative.

So you see, estate planning is actually a safe investment, not just for you but for those you care about. You will get more return (i.e., money saved for your estate) than what you put into it (i.e., the attorney's fees for setting up your opt-out strategy). It is also important to remember that there are different levels of opting out. For example, in earlier chapters we discussed how having a trust may provide better protection for your assets than just having a will. Well, there are also other tricks to protect your assets from taxes, both during your life and after you die.

Most wealthy people already know these tricks. Or, to be more accurate, they know enough to hire professionals who can help them understand the tricks. So the question remains, can average people also take advantage of tools the rich use to protect their estates? The answer is—and I am not trying to be intentionally vague here—*possibly*. You may also be thinking that if estate planning is such a great investment then a larger investment will save your estate even more money, right? Well, as with most legal questions, the answer is "it depends." This is because certain criteria must be met, based on wealth and the composition of that wealth. If they are met then, indeed, you will reap the benefits of a more comprehensive estate plan.

In this chapter, we're going to discuss some high-level estate planning. By high-level, I don't just mean the complexity of the documents and provisions therein but the composition of the family's estate. The higher the value, the more likely these double opt-out ideas will provide a larger return on investment.

Taxes

They say the only two guarantees in life are death and taxes. And as if that isn't depressing enough, you will also have to pay taxes *after* you die. How much depends on where you live and how much money you have; the wealthier you are, the more the government will try to skim money from the top before your heirs can claim it. Fortunately, the trend in most states has been to phase out the so-called "death tax" or do away with it altogether. Currently, California has no estate tax and has not had one since January 1, 2005. Even better, due to the structure of the state government, any attempt to reinstate it would have to be approved by the voters—and I think it's safe to say that's not going to happen any time soon. Go, California!

Of course, Californians still have to deal with the federal estate tax. As a result of the "fiscal cliff" debacle in early 2013, the government enacted the American Taxpayer Relief Act (ATRA). This law, among other things, made permanent the $5-million exemption for an individual's estate (plus increases for inflation). That means that at the current rates, individuals with $5.34 million or less (for 2014) will be exempt from the federal estate tax. If you have more than that amount, however, you will have to dish out a whopping 40 percent to the federal government. That alone is enough to kill you! Luckily, there are competent attorneys out there who can use the following tools to help you minimize your estate's tax burden.

Family Limited Partnership (FLP)

Business entities, such as corporations and partnerships, are afforded many protections and tax breaks that individuals are not. But did you know that you can turn your family business and possibly investments into a mini company for estate planning purposes? Well, you can, and it is known as a family limited partnership. The FLP is a very basic estate planning tool that allows families—particularly those with large real estate holdings or businesses—to move wealth from one generation to the next while they are alive but retain control. For example, a husband and wife want to give assets to their children without paying a ton of money in taxes. So they create a FLP and transfer the property or business into it. They appoint themselves general partners (GPs) who have all rights and responsibilities for managing the FLP's assets, thus retaining control. They make all decisions about the partnership's investments and activities.

The parents can then gift small percentages of that partnership to their children and grandchildren. However, the children are only limited partners (LPs), which means they cannot control the FLP in any way; they cannot even transfer their own interests to someone else (outside the family). They also carry limited liability.

There are several benefits to creating an FLP for all involved. The partnership is taxed as a "pass through" entity, which means that all partners report any income on their individual tax returns via a partnership K-1—there is no double taxation as with a C corporation.

Older family members (parents) can reduce their taxable estates with continued planned gifting of this partnership interest while remaining in control over their assets, which is very appealing to those in charge. Remember when we discussed the perils of giving lifetime gifts to one's children? Well, forming a FLP prevents many of these problems.

In addition, all partners of the FLP—whether they are general or limited partners—qualify for a fractional ownership discount; this is where death tax savings come in. A fractional ownership discount is recognized by the Internal Revenue Service and can reduce the appraised value of your estate when you die for the purposes of estate taxes. The lower your estate valuation, the lower your tax, which means that more money goes to your family instead of lining government coffers. By employing this sort of device, you can write your attorney *and* the IRS out of your estate. How's that for a win-win scenario?

Transfers of limited partnership interests are eligible for the annual gift tax exclusion, which is a powerful tool for reducing estate taxes. By law, the value of limited partnership shares can be discounted when transferred to family members, as well as at death. In addition, because of an FLP's flexibility, the family members who are owners can usually amend the partnership agreement as family circumstances change. This gives it an advantage over things such as joint tenancy and/or outright gifting.

One of the most important things an FLP does is shield the partners and the assets from future creditors and former spouses. Unlike lifetime gifts to one's children, creditors may not break the protection of the FLP. They cannot force cash distributions, vote, or own the interest of a limited partner without the consent of the general partners. And if there is an event in the family—such as a divorce—where a limited partner ceases to be a family member, the partnership documents can require a transfer back to the family for fair market value, thereby keeping the asset within the family structure.

An FLP allows a family to combine its investments, thereby reducing investment fees. For example, instead of having to maintain a separate brokerage account or property for each child, a FLP can have one account or combined real estate, and the children can own their shares as a partnership interest.

Intentionally Defective Grantor Trust

This type of trust is exactly how it sounds—it is written in such a way that it is intentionally defective. If you're like many of my clients, you're wondering why an attorney would create anything that is intentionally defective. The reason is that this allows us to pick and choose which terms we want to abide by and to adjust the outcomes and consequences of our actions so that the client gets the maximum benefit. It actually couldn't be less defective when considering that it operates exactly as planned. For example, the trust is created as a grantor trust; this means that the grantor (usually one or both parents) is the owner for tax purposes. So although they are gifting away the asset through the sale, it allows them to keep paying the taxes and receiving income. However, the defect means that when the grantor dies, the asset is no longer in the estate and therefore cannot be counted for estate tax purposes. This sort of device is effective for individuals who, as of the year 2014, have an estate of more than $5.34 million and couples with an estate of more than $10.68 million. With this sort of sophisticated estate planning tool, it is imperative that you seek the advice of a competent and experienced estate planning attorney who can not only properly prepare the initial documents for you but can also assist you on how to correctly administer the trust year after year.

Grantor Retained Annuity Trusts (GRATs)

This type of irrevocable trust has the potential to save your intended beneficiaries and/or heirs a whole lot of money. It has also become a very popular tool among the super-wealthy, including Facebook creator Mark Zuckerberg. Let's say you own stock in a company that you expect to increase rapidly in value. You can use a GRAT to keep the proceeds of that increase outside your taxable estate. The grantor transfers the property to the trust and, for a fixed number of years (usually a ten-year minimum), retains the right to receive a fixed annuity payment. After the time period ends, the trust property is distributed to the beneficiaries. If the grantor has survived the term, all property in the trust (as well as any interest generated by this property) is excluded from the estate for federal tax purposes.

There is a big downside to the GRAT, however: if the grantor dies during the annuity period, the entire trust property is included in his or her estate (and therefore subject to the estate tax). To avoid this pitfall, some estate planners have begun using a new method called a "guaranteed GRAT." To do this, they create the GRAT but add a provision that if the grantor dies during the period, the remaining assets revert to the estate (rather than going to the beneficiaries). This is referred to as "retaining a contingent reversion interest." Then, after the creating the GRAT, the grantor enters into an agreement with the beneficiaries, stating that they will purchase this contingent reversion interest at fair market value. The price is set at the time the agreement is created, which means it will likely be a lot less than what the beneficiaries would receive under the trust. It also means that if the grantor should die unexpectedly during the term, they will get the equivalent of the trust property tax-free. It is very important to note here that the legitimacy of guaranteed GRATs has not been upheld by California courts. Therefore, I highly recommend consulting an expert when considering this option.

Dynasty Trusts

These trusts are usually created by relatively wealthy people who want to ensure that their families *retain* their wealth for generations to come. This means minimizing the tax bill and ensuring that the trust assets cannot be touched by creditors, former spouses, or even the beneficiaries' wastefulness. A dynasty trust accomplishes all of these things.

The assets are only taxed one time—when they are placed in the trust. That means they are not subject to either the generation-skipping tax or gift tax that usually accompanies the transfer of wealth to each new generation of beneficiaries. Obviously, this saves the grantors' children, grandchildren, and so on enormous amounts of money over the years. Any revenue generated by trust assets *does* count as income for the beneficiaries' individual returns, so most grantors will fund the trust with assets that do not earn money, such as a life insurance policy.

Dynasty trusts are among the most complex estate planning tools. They are subject to several rules and regulations, including the Rule Against Perpetuities (whatever you do, don't try to understand this on your own—I have been told in confidence that many judges don't even fully understand this archaic rule, and it is even rendered moot by legislation in California). This rather old (and confusing) legal concept dictates how long the trust can continue. The basic premise of the rule is that it violates public policy to let one entity, individual, or—in this case—family own something for more than a certain amount of time. A dynasty trust, which can last indefinitely, would therefore be in violation of that policy.

While about half the states have gotten rid of the rule altogether, others—including California—have adopted the Uniform Statutory Rule Against Perpetuities. Essentially, this means a dynasty trust can last for about ninety years; after that, the trust is dissolved, and the assets are distributed to the beneficiaries. By that time, several generations of heirs have benefitted from enormous tax savings; it also prevents them from frivolously running through the family wealth or succumbing to the demands of their creditors.

There is, of course, a downside to dynasty trusts, and that is the lack of flexibility. They are irrevocable; the grantor makes the rules for the trust (e.g., how often beneficiaries get disbursements and what the money is to be used for), and they cannot be changed later on. That means that even if the family's circumstances have drastically changed, the grantor, trustee, and beneficiaries cannot break the trust. When someone chooses this type of trust, he or she is literally tying up the money for generations to come, based on his or her best guess on what will sustain the family in the coming years. As stated previously, seek advice from an expert before implementing this type of plan.

Irrevocable Life Insurance Trust

Life insurance can be an excellent vehicle for providing for your loved ones after your death. However, if you buy your own life insurance, the proceeds from the policy will be included in your estate for federal tax purposes—most people do not realize this. There is a way around it, though, with the creation of an irrevocable life insurance trust. It is easy enough to create. The trustor (you) sets up the trust, funds it (puts in money), and names the trustee and beneficiaries. The trustee then uses those funds to purchase the life insurance policy on the trustor's behalf. Upon the trustor's death, the proceeds go to the trust or directly to your beneficiaries, which gives them the liquidity to pay any death taxes due (as opposed to selling assets) or simply receive the proceeds as their inheritance.

If the trust has been properly created and managed, these funds will be exempt from federal estate taxes because the trust and/or beneficiaries owned the policy and not you. It was your initial gift that was taxed as a transfer and not the mature value of the policy. We can even continually fund the policy with an annual amount equal to the applicable annual exclusion (currently fourteen thousand dollars in 2014), and therefore you transfer wealth with no estate taxes. Pretty neat stuff, huh?

An irrevocable life insurance trust can be used to provide

the liquidity upon the death of the person who held the policy if he or she anticipated having a taxable estate. This liquidity often allows the heirs to hang on to assets after their parents pass away. All it takes is a little forethought and you can save hundreds of thousands, if not millions, of dollars in estate taxes.

I'll illustrate this point with an example from my own practice. One day, a new client came to my office; his parents had died in 2009, and he needed help with their estate. They had had the forethought to create a living trust; however, they had done so on the Internet without the advice of an attorney (you know where this is going). The client and his family had always lived a simple life, so it came as a complete shock to him that his mother and father had amassed a fortune of almost $10 million, mostly through the purchase of rental real estate. In fact, rent real estate comprised nearly the entire trust estate, and they were pretty cash poor.

As it turned out, the client's mother and father had passed away during the housing collapse, and, like most real estate at that time, its value was diminished (okay, more like decimated). Because they had not sought the advice of a competent estate planning attorney, they did not know about the benefits of an irrevocable life insurance trust. Such a vehicle could have been funded, thereby saving them millions of dollars. Instead, their son had to write a check to the IRS for $2.5 million in estate taxes. What's worse is that the family had to generate that cash by selling real estate when the market was at its lowest levels. A competent estate planning attorney could have advised them to use an irrevocable life insurance trust. Specifically, the mother and father would have taken out a "second to die" policy, with the proper amount funded to pay the estate taxes when they died. Yes, this would have been an expensive policy, but it certainly would have been less than the $2.5 million they had to pay in taxes, and they would have been able to generate the cash slowly rather than needing it all at once. This is a great example of how powerful these estate planning tools can be and why it is so important to seek the advice of an attorney, opt out of the government will, and continue to fine tune your plan to meet the evolving laws and changes in your wealth.

Oftentimes how you protect your assets depends on where you live. Remember that this book focuses on California law, which may be different from the law in New York, Idaho, or Florida. For example, the wealthy often use an asset protection trust—sometimes called a "self-settled spendthrift trust"—to protect themselves from creditors. A self-settled spendthrift trust is an irrevocable trust in which the trustor is also a beneficiary. The trustee, however, must be a third party; this way, he or she officially manages the trust and cannot be ordered by the court to disburse money to the trustor's creditors. This type of trust is not recognized in California, but that does not mean Californians cannot utilize it. They would have to create the trust in a state that allows such instruments, pick a trustee who is not under California jurisdiction, and exclude from the trust any property that is reachable by a California court, such as real estate located in the state. My point here is that it's important to speak to a competent attorney who can advise you of these nuances and protect your assets.

It's also important to remember that the law is always in flux, and these changes can have an enormous effect on your estate planning strategy. Right now, as you are reading this, bureaucrats, politicians, and lobbyists are brainstorming, drafting, and advocating laws that can impact all aspects of your life, including your finances. To illustrate this point, let's go back for a moment to the American Taxpayer Relief Act. During the "fiscal cliff" negotiations, there was a possibility of the death tax being increased greatly. Many lawmakers were in favor of this, as it would have increased tax revenue. That didn't happen, but had it gone the other way, there would have been a whole lot of people calling their attorneys to adjust their estate plans so they could avoid the increased tax. It's a lawyer's job to keep abreast not only of the current laws but the changing political winds that may affect them later on. He or she can help you sidestep the landmines and take advantage of benefits, whether you are a regular Joe or the wealthiest guy in town.

CHAPTER 10

Other Things to Consider

Most of the advice and scenarios in this book have been tailored to fit the typical situation: the average, "traditional" family with parents who want to secure their hard-earned assets for their children and ensure that their own end-of-life wishes are carried out. But what if you do not fit the typical situation? Perhaps you are unmarried, do not have kids, and do not own a home. I have found that these clients initially assume that because they have few assets or no heirs, they do not need to do any estate planning; however, they could not be more wrong. In fact, I contend that it may be even more important for them to have a well-thought-out and comprehensive estate plan.

Remember that when you die without a will, the state will follow its intestacy laws to decide who gets your estate. If you do not have a spouse or any blood relatives, the state will simply take your assets. In some states—including California—this is true even if you didn't live there at the time of your death. That includes real estate located in California, as well as personal property that was kept primarily in the state. Under certain circumstances, even intangible personal property may escheat to the state of California—this means your trademarks, patents, and other intellectual property. Now, even if you are not rich, you must have *something* you care about, something that you would rather go to trusted friends or a favorite charity rather than the state.

Also remember that this about more than just assets; it is also about your health care and end-of-life wishes. If you do not have any family members and you die or are incapacitated, do you want the state making decisions about your medical treatment or, God forbid, your funeral arrangements? Wouldn't you rather choose a trusted friend or life partner to make those decisions? If so, you need to engage in thorough estate planning.

Some people may even be worth more alive than dead. If you are a young person with a decent career or education and you're killed in a car accident, your estate will have a claim against the person (or their insurance) for your wrongful death. Your estate will get the award, which could be millions, and who knows who'll get that?

Protection for Non-Married Committed Couples

Let's say you found the love of your life; you live together, you share the bills, you go on vacations, you have a dog or perhaps even children together. The only thing you don't have is a piece of paper that says you're married (or in a domestic partnership). If you don't have that piece of paper, you'd better have an airtight estate plan that honors your relationship because the government won't. Instead, it will dispense with your assets strictly by the intestacy book.

Same-sex couples have been dealing with this issue for, well, forever. Their relationships were not considered legitimate under the law, so partners were unable to benefit from each other's estates; more importantly, they could not serve as next of kin to make medical decisions on each other's behalf. This was never more obvious than during the height of the AIDS crisis, when many partners were shut out of the medical decision-making process. Sometimes they were not even permitted to visit the sick person in the hospital, especially if the family didn't approve of the relationship.

Unmarried heterosexual couples have also dealt with this issue, albeit for less time. That's because in the olden days (a few decades ago), cohabitation outside of marriage carried a social stigma that prevented most people from living together before marriage. When things loosened up, socially speaking, unmarried heterosexual partners, at least those in California, found that they were treated much the same as same-sex couples.

That said, the estate planning process for unmarried couples is pretty much the same as it is for anyone else. It begins with a visit to a competent attorney whose practice focuses on estate planning and who understands the special needs of unmarried couples. From there, they should decide whether they want to draw up wills, create trusts, and perhaps take title to their home as joint tenants. Remember, though, that if they are joint tenants, each has to prepare their estate as if they will outlive the other and take full ownership under the right of survivorship (otherwise, as we said earlier, the property will end up in probate when the second partner dies). There is another caveat here as well. If your partner moved into your home and you decide to take title as joint tenants, you are giving that person a gift *now*. It's a gift that may be difficult to take back if the relationship ends badly so think long and hard about whether you want to take such a big step. Furthermore, gifting anyone any portion of real estate creates a gift for tax purposes, and therefore a gift tax return must be prepared.

I also caution my unmarried clients against relying solely on a will. That's because a will can more easily be contested, and when it is, it often leads to a long, drawn-out, and extremely expensive battle (remember that swarm of piranhas nipping away at your estate). Most of the time, the will is contested by family members who either disapproved of the relationship between the decedent and a particular beneficiary (i.e., romantic partner) or the decedent's life choices in general. If the family wins, your partner will be disinherited. That's why it makes much more sense to set up a revocable living trust naming him or her as the beneficiary. That way, if the relationship changes or ends, you can amend or terminate the trust. There is also the privacy issue; as I mentioned earlier, wills are a matter of public record, while trusts are administered privately.

So let's say that you have set up a trust for your partner, drawn up a will that leaves assets to him or her, and/or taken your home as joint tenants. Maybe you've even set pay-on-death or transfer-on-death designations for your bank accounts. You feel comfortable in the knowledge that your partner will be provided for in the event of your death. But you still have to take care of the most important thing: your health care. If in the event that you become ill or incapacitated, who do you want to be in charge of the medical and financial decisions? If it's your partner, you need to put that in writing through an advanced health care directive. This document will ensure that the person of your choosing can implement your health care and end-of-life wishes or make decisions about things you may not have thought of.

There is another important consideration for same-sex

couples that may impact their estate planning. Same-sex marriage continues to be a highly contentious issue throughout the country; however, in California, it seems to have finally been settled. After years of political back and forth, the Supreme Court held in *Hollingsworth v. Perry* (2013) that same-sex marriage is legal in California. This was undoubtedly a victory for LBGT advocates; however, it also brings up a host of legal issues of which same-sex couples, and those advising them, must be aware.

The Supreme Court's decision means that California will also recognize same-sex marriages performed in other states, as long as it is legal in that state. But this is not the law everywhere. Some states have not legalized same-sex marriages but will recognize them if they were performed in another state. Others will not recognize a same-sex marriage, no matter where it was performed. Sound confusing? Well, that's because it is. It also raises (at least) two red flags for same-sex couples considering marriage. The first is that a couple that comes to California for the purpose of getting married must make sure that their home state will recognize them as married (or prepare their estates accordingly); the second red flag is for California couples who own property in other states. In other words, if the couple owns property in a state with an amendment prohibiting same-sex marriage, what happens to that property when one of the spouses dies? I cannot venture to say what the outcome will be in this situation; I will only advise that you speak to a competent attorney in your state before you marry (or buy the property in another state). They may say you need to create additional testamentary documents to make sure your spouse gets the property.

Another very important issue that same-sex couples may have to consider is adoption. California has some of the nation's most liberal adoption laws for same-sex couples; however, there are loopholes that must be closed in the event of a partner's untimely death. For example, say a single woman gives birth to or adopts a child. She later meets and marries her partner, and that partner shares in all the childrearing duties. If the adoptive parent dies, the second parent will have no legal right to that child, no matter how close they have become. The second partner would have had to legally adopt the child (second parent adoption), or the adoptive parent would have had to create an estate plan that named her spouse as the guardian.

Finally, if you already have a domestic partnership with your future spouse, you do not have to dissolve the partnership before you marry. However, if you have a domestic partnership with a *previous* partner, you must dissolve that before you marry your present partner. The important thing, as always, is to consult a family law attorney or estate planner who has expertise in resolving issues for same-sex couples.

Providing for Your Pets

In 2011, an Italian woman named Maria Assunta died at the age of ninety-four. News of her death made headlines around the world, not because she was famous but because she left her entire estate, all €10 million ($13.5 million) of it, to her cat, Tommaso, a former stray on the streets of Rome. Assunta had taken him in and, upon her death, made him the third-richest cat in the world. Yes, I said third-richest cat, which means there are at least two other cats with net worths over $10 million. Frightening.

As Italian law does not permit someone to leave money directly to an animal, the millions were left in a trust to be administered by Ms. Assunta's former caregiver. No one, including the caregiver, had known how wealthy the woman was, as she had lived a very simple life. She had survived her husband and had no children, but apparently Tommaso meant the world to her.

Right now you're probably thinking that Ms. Assunta was crazy as well as rich, but whatever the case, the story is not all that uncommon. Many people consider their pets to be very important members of their family, and they worry about what will happen to their furry friends in the event of their death or incapacitation. If they have the government will, they have good reason to be concerned. As with all other testamentary intentions, the government does not care about what will happen to your pets if you pass away.

Animals are not part of the intestacy laws; rather, they are considered personal property, and if no one wants them, they will be taken to a shelter—possibly even a kill shelter.

Many people think of pets as having purely sentimental value, but some animals have significant monetary value as well. Think of horses, trained guard dogs, and breeding livestock. All of these assets are in the same class as pets and are considered personal property despite having significant value. Yes, some people are very attached to these high-priced animals as well, but the point here is that some pets are expensive and can cost an estate if not accounted for in the estate plan.

Providing for your pets through estate planning is two-fold: you need to choose who you would like to care for them (this is actually similar to designating a guardian for your children), and you most likely need to set aside funds specifically for the pet's care. These funds will be under the control of the trustee. This person can be the same as the one who will care for the animal; however, many attorneys and estate planners will advise you to choose two different people to fill these roles. You can also choose a financial institution to administer the funds. The point is you want to make certain the money is actually being used for the pet's needs, and a separate trustee can provide that oversight.

If you don't have anyone you trust to care for your pet, another option is to designate a no-kill shelter as the recipient. You would simply instruct the trustee to take your pet to a shelter that does not euthanize animals; this way, you are assured your pet will not be a victim. Furthermore, I often advise my clients to include a donation to the shelter that takes their pet. Nothing is more likely to give your pet a warm welcome than a check for five thousand dollars tucked under its collar!

There are two different types of pet trusts. One is a testamentary trust, which is part of your will or trust and therefore takes effect upon your death. This trust outlines everything a caregiver will need to know about your pet—what it likes to eat, how it likes to play, whether it has any health conditions or medications that need to be administered, and its daily routine. It also includes special instructions, such as whether your dog should wear a muzzle before going out in public. The trustee (if separate from the caregiver) administers the funds and makes sure they are being used to care for the pet per the testator's instructions.

The second type of trust was created by statute, hence the name "statutory pet trust." It falls under the California probate code, which requires the trustee to honor the terms of the trust. Basically, it took the duties the trustee already had and made them official. In the legal world, this means that when they are not carried out, there are consequences. The statute gives third parties the right to challenge the trust if the trustee is not fulfilling his or her duties and gives the court the power to appoint a new trustee so that the wishes of the settler (the person who created the trust) are carried out to the letter.

Say, for example, that you create a pet trust to provide for the care of your dog, Sammi. Your best friend, Sheila, is a fellow animal lover and has known Sammi since she was a puppy. And because Sheila has always been such a good friend, you make her both the caregiver and the trustee. The trust includes specific instructions on how Sammi is to be cared for, including the fact that your Aunt Josie (who Sammi has always loved) is authorized to visit Sammi and take her for a walk three times a week.

After your death, Sheila brings Sammi to her home, and because she is also the trustee, she has access to the trust funds. Everything's great, right? Well, no, because whenever your Aunt Josie tries to arrange a visit, Sheila makes excuses or ignores the calls altogether. When Aunt Josie stops by unannounced, Sammi's tail is down and she looks like she has not been groomed in months. Under the statute, Aunt Josie can challenge Sheila's right to remain trustee, and if the court agrees that she is not upholding her duties, it can replace her. For this reason, a lot of people choose the statutory trust over the testamentary trust.

Another reason they choose the statutory trust is that, like other living trusts, it takes effect as soon as you create it. During your lifetime, you can fund it as you see fit and make any other necessary changes. On the other hand, if you include the trust in your will, the funds will not be available until the end of the probate process. In the meantime, your caregiver will have to lay out the money for your pet's care, which may pose a hardship for the caregiver and your pet.

So how much money should you put in the pet trust? It depends on the size of your estate, the type of pet you have, the standard of living your pet is used to, how many pets you have, and how long those pets are expected to live. You must take into account food and medical expenses for the life of your pet. Generally, it is advisable to put twice as much as you think your pet(s) will need. Also, please note that while a court (in California) cannot reduce the amount of the trust, your other beneficiaries (who are probably angry that you left so much money to a dog) can try to fight it.

What if your pet dies and there is still money left in the trust? You want to be sure to designate who will receive any surplus, whether that be charities, friends, or relatives.

YOUR ESTATE PLANNING SUPPORT SYSTEM

Throughout this book, I have been talking about all the estate planning tools you can use to opt out of the government will, avoid probate, and save your hard-earned assets for your friends, families, and charities. However, these tools are not much use unless the person drawing them up has knowledge of the legal subtleties involved or if the people you choose to administer your estate are unscrupulous or unmotivated. It is therefore of paramount importance that you use due diligence when choosing your estate planning support group.

Choosing the Right Attorney

All throughout this text, I've been cautioning you to engage a competent attorney to prepare your documents. However, it is just as important that you engage the right *kind* of attorney. Think of it this way: would you want a heart surgeon to perform surgery on your brain? The principle is the same—you want to find an attorney who focuses his or her practice on estate planning. There are many nuances—and, therefore, many pitfalls—involved in estate planning, so whoever you hire must be intimately familiar with these. One incorrectly prepared document can completely change the estate plan and land the entire family in court. This is illustrated by the following example.

One day, a young man named Adam walked into my office asking for my help. You see, Adam had a friend—we'll call her Sally. Sally—who was around ninety years old, but despite the huge age gap between them, the two had been close friends for many years. They were so close, in fact, that she wanted to leave Adam a very generous gift in her will. As it turned out, Sally had significant wealth, which she shared with her undeserving five children. Sally was a very generous woman, even to a fault. She had made lifetime gifts to her children and had left them the entirety of her estate through her will. However, she did have one piece of property that her young friend Adam had helped her manage, and it was her wish that Adam would receive this property when she died.

This was not a case in which someone neglected to engage in planning; on the contrary, Sally had a rather complex estate plan. The problem was that the attorney she chose failed to prepare a document that was very crucial, given the relationship between Adam and Sally. You see, Adam used to take care of Sally, not because he had to, not because he was paid to, but because he wanted to. Adam was a recovering alcoholic, and Sally had saved his life by helping him get sober and find meaning in his life again. Unfortunately, it was this two-way, reciprocal relationship that ultimately led to his not getting what Sally wanted him to have. The State of California has a very broad definition of the term "caregiver"; California's probate code also disqualifies caregivers from receiving gifts. Adam's treatment of Sally brought him squarely within that definition; therefore, he would be unable to receive a bequest from his good friend Sally. This law was actually created for a very important reason: to protect vulnerable seniors from unscrupulous caregivers who are trying to steal from them. Unfortunately, good people like Adam often fall victim to it.

In California, when a client wants to make a gift to a caregiver, I must complete a form called a certificate of independent review. Basically, this allows another attorney—the independent reviewer—to look over your estate plan and authorize your gift to a caregiver. Most estate planning attorneys will do this if there is even a remote possibly that someone receiving a gift will be considered a caregiver; it is better to be safe than sorry. Had Sally gone to a more thorough attorney, a certificate of independent review would have allowed Adam to receive his gift. Instead, Sally's five children sued the estate and won; Adam got nothing, and Sally's intentions regarding the disposition of her estate were not honored. It is stories like this that demonstrate how important it is to choose a competent estate planner to help you.

Timing

It is not only important to opt out of the government will; it's also important to do so in a timely fashion. A lot of people hem and haw right until the end, which is something I highly discourage, as it leaves too much room for errors and unanswered questions. For example, I recently had a client who for over a year had known he had terminal cancer, yet he waited until he was very close to death before engaging in estate planning. Now, although we did everything we could to prepare the estate plan within hours (literally—we did it within forty-eight hours, from the meeting to the signing of documents, which was pretty amazing), there were still inherent issues that could not be resolved within such a short time. The client had property out of state, and because I am licensed in California, I could not transfer property in from another state. We contacted a title company in the state where the property was located, but unfortunately my client died before we could move the property into the trust. In the end, we were stuck doing a probate in another state in the trust administration in California, thus doubling the fees and causing a lot of headaches to his surviving spouse.

While this example concerns a client who knew he was going to die, it is just as important for healthy people to create their estate plans sooner rather than later. I am not trying to scare anyone here, just stating a simple yet often uncomfortable truth: anything can happen at any time, and we need to protect our beneficiaries.

Picking a Trustee

The majority of my practice deals with preparation—setting up an estate so that things run smoothly after the client's death. I do everything I can to avoid litigation, but unfortunately there is no way to eliminate the risk completely. When my office does have to deal with litigation, it usually has to do with the trustees of a trust: the beneficiaries have a dispute with the trustees, the trustees have disputes with each other, or the trustees just do something plain wrong. Most of the time, however, they *are* doing the right thing and are just not getting along with another party. For this reason, I usually spend a lot of time discussing with my clients who should serve as the successor trustee for their trusts. We currently have a case in which the decedent chose a poor trustee. This trustee did not have the skills that it takes to keep people working together and keep the administration simple. The result was a lot of hard feelings, as well as higher fees incurred by several attorneys playing referee to the administrative squabbles. Now, I never met the decedent in this case, but I'm quite sure she did not want her family fighting over her estate and a bunch of attorneys getting rich from it.

There is a common misconception that trustees need to have business acumen, know about the stock market, and understand real estate transactions. This couldn't be further from the truth. The bottom line is you want a trustee that you can—you ready for it?—*trust*. Yes, trustworthiness is the most important quality they should have. This is because trustees can hire an attorney, a CPA, a realtor, a financial advisor, or any other professional to assist them in managing the estate; they don't need to have these skills themselves. I mean, who does know all that stuff anyway? If trustees had to meet those kinds of requirements, no one would ever get the job (and no one would want it, either!). What trustees need to be are trusted, trustworthy, and trustable. Sensing a theme here? These qualities give you the confidence that they will follow your directions, no matter what they may be. And that is what is important.

In Summation

Throughout this book, I have done my best to help you begin navigating the complex and often convoluted land known as wills and estates law. This is not a self-help or how-to guide; instead, I like to think of it as food for thought, the spark that makes you start thinking about estate planning in a different way.

My first goal was to shed some light on the government will so you realize that it's in your best interest to opt out of it. My second goal was to explain why you should not engage in estate planning on your own but seek out an experienced estate planning attorney to help you (and to arm you with the right questions to ask when you walk into his or her office). What's most important to me, however, is that everyone realizes their personal power. Throughout our lives, we are obligated to submit to the government; we pay taxes and (hopefully) follow its laws, and for this we reap many great benefits. But that does not mean we should turn over control of our assets, health care, and end-of-life decisions to the government when we die. These assets are our life's work, and they should go to the people or organizations we care about most. Decisions regarding medical care and funeral arrangements should be left in the hands of those who love us and respect our wishes. These wishes are a reflection of who we are and how we lived, and they deserve to be honored. This book may focus on the laws of California, but its principles hold true no matter where you live. That said, I will leave you with the words I often tell my clients:

FAILING TO PLAN IS PLANNING TO FAIL.

Visit us at www.GullottaLaw.com.

www.ingramcontent.com/pod-product-compliance
Lightning Source LLC
LaVergne TN
LVHW051839080426
835512LV00018B/2967